OFFICIAL SQA PAST PAPERS WITH ANSWERS

HIGHER

MATHEMATICS
2007-2011

Publisher's Note

We are delighted to bring you the 2011 Past Papers and you will see that we have changed the format from previous editions. As part of our environmental awareness strategy, we have attempted to make these new editions as sustainable as possible.

To do this, we have printed on white paper and bound the answer sections into the book. This not only allows us to use significantly less paper but we are also, for the first time, able to source all the materials from sustainable sources.

We hope you like the new editions and by purchasing this product, you are not only supporting an independent Scottish publishing company but you are also, in the International Year of Forests, not contributing to the destruction of the world's forests.

Thank you for your support and please see the following websites for more information to support the above statement –

www.fsc-uk.org

www.loveforests.com

© Scottish Qualifications Authority
All rights reserved. Copying prohibited. No part of this publication may be reproduced, stored in a retrieval system, or transmitted in any form or by any means, electronic, mechanical, photocopying, recording or otherwise.

First exam published in 2007.
Published by Bright Red Publishing Ltd, 6 Stafford Street, Edinburgh EH3 7AU
tel: 0131 220 5804 fax: 0131 220 6710 info@brightredpublishing.co.uk www.brightredpublishing.co.uk

ISBN 978-1-84948-221-9

A CIP Catalogue record for this book is available from the British Library.

Bright Red Publishing is grateful to the copyright holders, as credited on the final page of the Question Section, for permission to use their material. Every effort has been made to trace the copyright holders and to obtain their permission for the use of copyright material. Bright Red Publishing will be happy to receive information allowing us to rectify any error or omission in future editions.

Please be aware that the format of the
Higher Mathematics examination changed
in 2008. Although the 2007 examination
paper is no longer in the required format, the
course content is unchanged and you will still
find these questions to be useful exam practice.

[BLANK PAGE]

X100/301

| NATIONAL
QUALIFICATIONS
2007 | TUESDAY, 15 MAY
9.00 AM – 10.10 AM | MATHEMATICS
HIGHER
Units 1, 2 and 3
Paper 1
(Non-calculator) |

Read Carefully

1 **Calculators may <u>NOT</u> be used in this paper.**

2 Full credit will be given only where the solution contains appropriate working.

3 Answers obtained by readings from scale drawings will not receive any credit.

SCOTTISH
QUALIFICATIONS
AUTHORITY

FORMULAE LIST

Circle:

The equation $x^2 + y^2 + 2gx + 2fy + c = 0$ represents a circle centre $(-g, -f)$ and radius $\sqrt{g^2 + f^2 - c}$.

The equation $(x - a)^2 + (y - b)^2 = r^2$ represents a circle centre (a, b) and radius r.

Scalar Product: $a.b = |a|\,|b|\cos\theta$, where θ is the angle between a and b

or $a.b = a_1b_1 + a_2b_2 + a_3b_3$ where $a = \begin{pmatrix} a_1 \\ a_2 \\ a_3 \end{pmatrix}$ and $b = \begin{pmatrix} b_1 \\ b_2 \\ b_3 \end{pmatrix}$.

Trigonometric formulae:

$$\sin(A \pm B) = \sin A \cos B \pm \cos A \sin B$$
$$\cos(A \pm B) = \cos A \cos B \mp \sin A \sin B$$
$$\sin 2A = 2\sin A \cos A$$
$$\cos 2A = \cos^2 A - \sin^2 A$$
$$= 2\cos^2 A - 1$$
$$= 1 - 2\sin^2 A$$

Table of standard derivatives:

$f(x)$	$f'(x)$
$\sin ax$	$a\cos ax$
$\cos ax$	$-a\sin ax$

Table of standard integrals:

$f(x)$	$\int f(x)\,dx$
$\sin ax$	$-\dfrac{1}{a}\cos ax + C$
$\cos ax$	$\dfrac{1}{a}\sin ax + C$

ALL questions should be attempted.

Marks

1. Find the equation of the line through the point (–1, 4) which is parallel to the line with equation $3x - y + 2 = 0$.

    3

2. Relative to a suitable coordinate system A and B are the points (–2, 1, –1) and (1, 3, 2) respectively.

    A, B and C are collinear points and C is positioned such that BC = 2AB.

    Find the coordinates of C.

    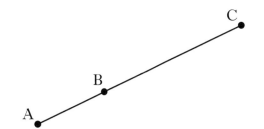

    4

3. Functions f and g, defined on suitable domains, are given by $f(x) = x^2 + 1$ and $g(x) = 1 - 2x$.

    Find:

    (a) $g(f(x))$;

    2

    (b) $g(g(x))$.

    2

4. Find the range of values of k such that the equation $kx^2 - x - 1 = 0$ has no real roots.

    4

5. The large circle has equation $x^2 + y^2 - 14x - 16y + 77 = 0$.

    Three congruent circles with centres A, B and C are drawn inside the large circle with the centres lying on a line parallel to the x-axis.

    This pattern is continued, as shown in the diagram.

    Find the equation of the circle with centre D.

    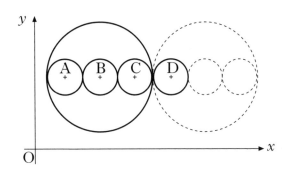

    5

[Turn over

Marks

6. Solve the equation $\sin 2x° = 6\cos x°$ for $0 \leq x \leq 360$.   **4**

7. A sequence is defined by the recurrence relation

$$u_{n+1} = \frac{1}{4}u_n + 16, \ u_0 = 0.$$

(a) Calculate the values of u_1, u_2 and u_3.   **3**

Four terms of this sequence, u_1, u_2, u_3 and u_4 are plotted as shown in the graph.

As $n \to \infty$, the points on the graph approach the line $u_n = k$, where k is the limit of this sequence.

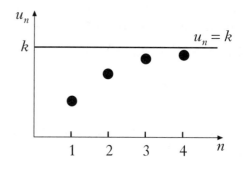

(b) (i) Give a reason why this sequence has a limit.

(ii) Find the exact value of k.   **3**

8. The diagram shows a sketch of the graph of $y = x^3 - 4x^2 + x + 6$.

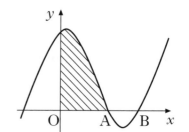

(a) Show that the graph cuts the x-axis at $(3, 0)$.   **1**

(b) Hence or otherwise find the coordinates of A.   **3**

(c) Find the shaded area.   **5**

9. A function f is defined by the formula $f(x) = 3x - x^3$.

(a) Find the exact values where the graph of $y = f(x)$ meets the x- and y-axes.   **2**

(b) Find the coordinates of the stationary points of the function and determine their nature.   **7**

(c) Sketch the graph of $y = f(x)$.   **1**

Marks

10. Given that $y = \sqrt{3x^2 + 2}$, find $\dfrac{dy}{dx}$.

    3

11. (a) Express $f(x) = \sqrt{3}\cos x + \sin x$ in the form $k\cos(x - a)$, where $k > 0$ and $0 < a < \dfrac{\pi}{2}$.

    4

    (b) Hence or otherwise sketch the graph of $y = f(x)$ in the interval $0 \leq x \leq 2\pi$.

    4

[END OF QUESTION PAPER]

[BLANK PAGE]

X100/303

NATIONAL QUALIFICATIONS 2007	TUESDAY, 15 MAY 10.30 AM – 12.00 NOON	**MATHEMATICS** HIGHER Units 1, 2 and 3 Paper 2

Read Carefully

1 **Calculators may be used in this paper.**

2 Full credit will be given only where the solution contains appropriate working.

3 Answers obtained by readings from scale drawings will not receive any credit.

SCOTTISH QUALIFICATIONS AUTHORITY

©

FORMULAE LIST

Circle:

The equation $x^2 + y^2 + 2gx + 2fy + c = 0$ represents a circle centre $(-g, -f)$ and radius $\sqrt{g^2 + f^2 - c}$.

The equation $(x - a)^2 + (y - b)^2 = r^2$ represents a circle centre (a, b) and radius r.

Scalar Product: $a.b = |a|\,|b| \cos \theta$, where θ is the angle between a and b

or $a.b = a_1b_1 + a_2b_2 + a_3b_3$ where $a = \begin{pmatrix} a_1 \\ a_2 \\ a_3 \end{pmatrix}$ and $b = \begin{pmatrix} b_1 \\ b_2 \\ b_3 \end{pmatrix}$.

Trigonometric formulae:

$$\sin (A \pm B) = \sin A \cos B \pm \cos A \sin B$$
$$\cos (A \pm B) = \cos A \cos B \mp \sin A \sin B$$
$$\sin 2A = 2\sin A \cos A$$
$$\cos 2A = \cos^2 A - \sin^2 A$$
$$= 2\cos^2 A - 1$$
$$= 1 - 2\sin^2 A$$

Table of standard derivatives:

$f(x)$	$f'(x)$
$\sin ax$	$a \cos ax$
$\cos ax$	$-a \sin ax$

Table of standard integrals:

$f(x)$	$\int f(x)\,dx$
$\sin ax$	$-\dfrac{1}{a} \cos ax + C$
$\cos ax$	$\dfrac{1}{a} \sin ax + C$

ALL questions should be attempted.

Marks

1. OABCDEFG is a cube with side 2 units, as shown in the diagram.

    B has coordinates (2, 2, 0).

    P is the centre of face OCGD and Q is the centre of face CBFG.

    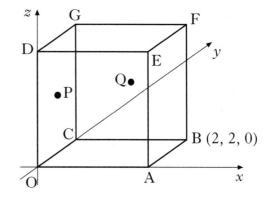

    (a) Write down the coordinates of G.   **1**

    (b) Find **p** and **q**, the position vectors of points P and Q.   **2**

    (c) Find the size of angle POQ.   **5**

2. The diagram shows two right-angled triangles with angles c and d marked as shown.

    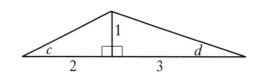

    (a) Find the exact value of $\sin(c + d)$.   **4**

    (b) (i) Find the exact value of $\sin 2c$.

         (ii) Show that $\cos 2d$ has the same exact value.   **4**

3. Show that the line with equation $y = 6 - 2x$ is a tangent to the circle with equation $x^2 + y^2 + 6x - 4y - 7 = 0$ and find the coordinates of the point of contact of the tangent and the circle.   **6**

4. The diagram shows part of the graph of a function whose equation is of the form $y = a\sin(bx^\circ) + c$.

    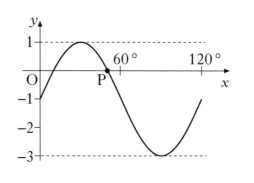

    (a) Write down the values of a, b and c.   **3**

    (b) Determine the exact value of the x-coordinate of P, the point where the graph intersects the x-axis as shown in the diagram.   **3**

[Turn over

Marks

5. A circle centre C is situated so that it touches the parabola with equation $y = \frac{1}{2}x^2 - 8x + 34$ at P and Q.

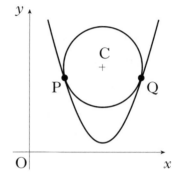

   (a) The gradient of the tangent to the parabola at Q is 4. Find the coordinates of Q. **5**

   (b) Find the coordinates of P. **2**

   (c) Find the coordinates of C, the centre of the circle. **2**

6. A householder has a garden in the shape of a right-angled isosceles triangle.

   It is intended to put down a section of rectangular wooden decking at the side of the house, as shown in the diagram.

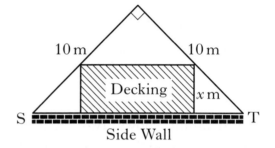

   (a) (i) Find the exact value of ST.

   (ii) Given that the breadth of the decking is x metres, show that the area of the decking, A square metres, is given by

   $$A = \left(10\sqrt{2}\right)x - 2x^2.$$ **3**

   (b) Find the dimensions of the decking which maximises its area. **5**

7. Find the value of $\int_0^2 \sin(4x + 1)\, dx$. **4**

8. The curve with equation $y = \log_3(x - 1) - 2 \cdot 2$, where $x > 1$, cuts the x-axis at the point $(a, 0)$.

   Find the value of a. **4**

Marks

9. The diagram shows the graph of $y = a^x$, $a > 1$.

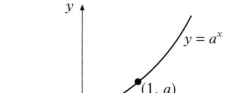

   On separate diagrams, sketch the graphs of:

   (a) $y = a^{-x}$; **2**

   (b) $y = a^{1-x}$. **2**

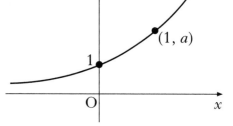

10. The diagram shows the graphs of a cubic function $y = f(x)$ and its derived function $y = f'(x)$.

    Both graphs pass through the point $(0, 6)$.

    The graph of $y = f'(x)$ also passes through the points $(2, 0)$ and $(4, 0)$.

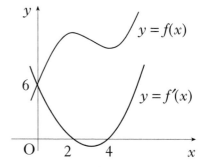

    (a) Given that $f'(x)$ is of the form $k(x - a)(x - b)$:

       (i) write down the values of a and b;

       (ii) find the value of k. **3**

    (b) Find the equation of the graph of the cubic function $y = f(x)$. **4**

11. Two variables x and y satisfy the equation $y = 3 \times 4^x$.

    (a) Find the value of a if $(a, 6)$ lies on the graph with equation $y = 3 \times 4^x$. **1**

    (b) If $(-\frac{1}{2}, b)$ also lies on the graph, find b. **1**

    (c) A graph is drawn of $\log_{10} y$ against x. Show that its equation will be of the form $\log_{10} y = Px + Q$ and state the gradient of this line. **4**

[*END OF QUESTION PAPER*]

[BLANK PAGE]

[BLANK PAGE]

[C100/SQP321]

Mathematics
Higher
Paper 1
Specimen Question Paper
(for examinations from Diet 2008 onwards)

NATIONAL
QUALIFICATIONS

Read carefully

Calculators may <u>NOT</u> be used in this paper.

Section A – Questions 1–20 (40 marks)

Instructions for completion of **Section A** are given on page two.

For this section of the examination you must use an **HB pencil**.

Section B (30 marks)

1   Full credit will be given only where the solution contains appropriate working.

2   Answers obtained by readings from scale drawings will not receive any credit.

SCOTTISH
QUALIFICATIONS
AUTHORITY

Read carefully

1 Check that the answer sheet provided is for **Mathematics Higher (Section A)**.

2 For this section of the examination you must use an **HB pencil** and, where necessary, an eraser.

3 Check that the answer sheet you have been given has **your name**, **date of birth**, **SCN** (Scottish Candidate Number) and **Centre Name** printed on it.

   Do not change any of these details.

4 If any of this information is wrong, tell the Invigilator immediately.

5 If this information is correct, **print** your name and seat number in the boxes provided.

6 The answer to each question is **either** A, B, C or D. Decide what your answer is, then, using your pencil, put a horizontal line in the space provided (see sample question below).

7 There is **only one correct** answer to each question.

8 Rough working should **not** be done on your answer sheet.

9 At the end of the exam, put the **answer sheet for Section A inside the front cover of your answer book**.

Sample Question

A curve has equation $y = x^3 - 4x$.

What is the gradient at the point where $x = 2$?

   A   8

   B   1

   C   0

   D −4

The correct answer is **A**—8. The answer **A** has been clearly marked in **pencil** with a horizontal line (see below).

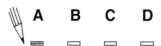

Changing an answer

If you decide to change your answer, carefully erase your first answer and using your pencil, fill in the answer you want. The answer below has been changed to **D**.

FORMULAE LIST

Circle:

The equation $x^2 + y^2 + 2gx + 2fy + c = 0$ represents a circle centre $(-g, -f)$ and radius $\sqrt{g^2 + f^2 - c}$.

The equation $(x - a)^2 + (y - b)^2 = r^2$ represents a circle centre (a, b) and radius r.

Scalar Product: $\mathbf{a}.\mathbf{b} = |\mathbf{a}|\,|\mathbf{b}| \cos \theta$, where θ is the angle between $\mathbf{a}$ and $\mathbf{b}$

or $\mathbf{a}.\mathbf{b} = a_1 b_1 + a_2 b_2 + a_3 b_3$ where $\mathbf{a} = \begin{pmatrix} a_1 \\ a_2 \\ a_3 \end{pmatrix}$ and $\mathbf{b} = \begin{pmatrix} b_1 \\ b_2 \\ b_3 \end{pmatrix}$.

Trigonometric formulae:

$$\sin(A \pm B) = \sin A \cos B \pm \cos A \sin B$$
$$\cos(A \pm B) = \cos A \cos B \mp \sin A \sin B$$
$$\sin 2A = 2\sin A \cos A$$
$$\cos 2A = \cos^2 A - \sin^2 A$$
$$= 2\cos^2 A - 1$$
$$= 1 - 2\sin^2 A$$

Table of standard derivatives:

$f(x)$	$f'(x)$
$\sin ax$	$a \cos ax$
$\cos ax$	$-a \sin ax$

Table of standard integrals:

$f(x)$	$\int f(x)\,dx$
$\sin ax$	$-\dfrac{1}{a}\cos ax + C$
$\cos ax$	$\dfrac{1}{a}\sin ax + C$

SECTION A

ALL questions should be attempted.

1. If $y = \dfrac{x^3 - x}{x^2}$, what is $\dfrac{dy}{dx}$?

  A $\dfrac{3x^2 - 1}{2x}$

  B $1 + \dfrac{1}{x^2}$

  C $\dfrac{3}{2}x - \dfrac{1}{2}$

  D $x^3 - x - x^{-2}$

2. Functions f and g are given by $f(x) = 2x - 3$ and $g(x) = x^2$.

Find an expression for $g(f(x))$.

  A $g(f(x)) = 4x^2 - 12x + 9$

  B $g(f(x)) = x^2 + 2x - 3$

  C $g(f(x)) = 4x - 9$

  D $g(f(x)) = 2x^3 - 3x^2$

3. Find $\displaystyle\int \dfrac{1}{\sqrt[3]{x}}\, dx$.

  A $-\dfrac{3}{2}x^{-\frac{1}{2}} + c$

  B $x^{-3} + c$

  C $\dfrac{3}{2}x^{\frac{2}{3}} + c$

  D $-2x^{-2} + c$

4.   A and B have coordinates $(2, 3, -2)$ and $(-1, -4, 0)$ respectively.

What is the distance between A and B?

A $\sqrt{6}$

B $\sqrt{17}$

C $\sqrt{62}$

D $\sqrt{148}$

5.   A sequence is defined by the recurrence relation

$$u_{n+1} = 3u_n - 4, \ u_0 = -1.$$

What is the value of u_2?

A -25

B -10

C -4

D -1

6. The diagram shows a sketch of $y = f(x)$.

Which of the diagrams below shows a sketch of $y = -3 - f(x)$?

A

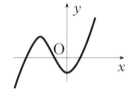

B

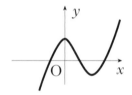

C

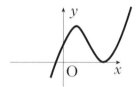

D

7. Which of the following describes the stationary point on the curve with equation $y = 3(x - 4)^2 - 5$?

    A   minimum at $(4, 5)$

    B   maximum at $(4, 5)$

    C   minimum at $(4, -5)$

    D   maximum at $(4, -5)$

8. The diagram shows a right-angled triangle with sides of 1, $2\sqrt{2}$ and 3.

What is the value of $\sin 2x°$?

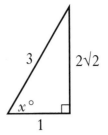

A $\dfrac{4\sqrt{2}}{9}$

B $\sqrt{\dfrac{2}{3}}$

C $\dfrac{4\sqrt{2}}{3}$

D $\dfrac{3}{\sqrt{2}}$

9. a and b are angles as shown in the diagram.

What is the value of $\sin(a - b)$?

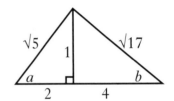

A $-\dfrac{7}{\sqrt{85}}$

B $\dfrac{2}{\sqrt{85}}$

C $\dfrac{1}{\sqrt{5}} + \dfrac{1}{\sqrt{17}}$

D $\dfrac{1}{\sqrt{5}} - \dfrac{1}{\sqrt{17}}$

10. A circle has equation $x^2 + y^2 + 8x - 6y - 12 = 0$.

What is the radius of this circle?

A $\sqrt{2}$

B $\sqrt{19}$

C $\sqrt{37}$

D $\sqrt{88}$

11. The points P(1, 3, 7), Q(5, 13, 13) and R(s, 33, 25) are collinear as shown in the diagram.

What is the value of s?

A   9

B   10

C   13

D   31

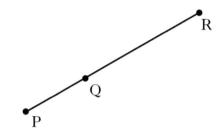

12. If $2x^2 - 12x + 11$ is expressed in the form $2(x - b)^2 + c$, what is the value of c?

A   −25

B   −7

C   11

D   23

13. The curve $y = f(x)$ is such that $\dfrac{dy}{dx} = 3x^2 + 9x + 1$ and the curve passes through the origin.

What is the equation of the curve?

A $y = x^3 + \dfrac{9}{2}x^2 + x$

B $y = 6x^3 + 9x^2$

C $y = 3x^3 + 9x^2 + x + 1$

D $y = 6x + 9$

14. For what value of k does the equation $x^2 - 3x + k = 0$ have equal roots?

A $-\dfrac{9}{4}$

B $-\dfrac{1}{12}$

C 0

D $\dfrac{9}{4}$

15. The point P(–1, 2) lies on the circle with equation $x^2 + y^2 - 6x - 8y + 5 = 0$.

What is the gradient of the tangent at P?

A -2

B $-\dfrac{1}{3}$

C $\dfrac{6}{7}$

D $\dfrac{1}{2}$

16. What is the value of $\displaystyle\int_{0}^{\frac{\pi}{6}} 4\cos 2x\,dx$?

A -2

B $-\sqrt{\dfrac{3}{2}}$

C $\sqrt{3}$

D 4

17. The graph shown in the diagram has equation of the form $y = \sin(px) + q$.

What are the values of p and q?

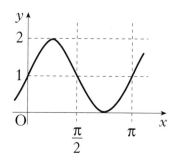

	p	q
A	2	1
B	$\frac{1}{2}$	1
C	2	2
D	$\frac{1}{2}$	2

18. The vectors a, b and c are represented by the sides of a right-angled triangle as shown in the diagram.

$|a| = 3$ and $|c| = 5$.

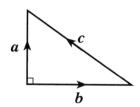

Here are two statements about these vectors:

    (1) $a.c = 9$

    (2) $a.b = -1$

Which of the following is true?

A   neither statement is correct

B   only statement (1) is correct

C   only statement (2) is correct

D   both statements are correct

19. If $\log_3 t = 2 + \log_3 5$, what is the value of t?

A   7

B   10

C   25

D   45

20. If $3^k = e^4$, find an expression for k.

A $k = \sqrt[3]{4^e}$

B $k = \dfrac{e^4}{3}$

C $k = 4 / \log_e 3$

D $k = 1 / \log_e 3$

[*END OF SECTION A*]

SECTION B

ALL questions should be attempted.

Marks

21. A firm cleans the factory floor on a daily basis with disinfectant. It has a choice of two products, either "A" or "B".

    Product A removes 70% of all germs but during the next 24 hours, 300 "new" germs per sq unit are estimated to appear.

    Product B removes 80% of all germs but during the next 24 hours, 350 "new" germs per sq unit are estimated to appear.

    For product A, let u_n represent the number of germs per sq unit on the floor immediately before disinfecting for the nth time.

    For product B, let v_n represent the number of germs per sq unit on the floor immediately before disinfecting for the nth time.

    (a) Write down a recurrence relation for each product to show the number of germs per sq unit present prior to disinfecting.　　2

    (b) Determine which product is more effective in the long term.　　4

22. (a) Find the stationary points on the curve with equation $y = x^3 - 9x^2 + 24x - 20$ and justify their nature.　　7

    (b) (i) Show that $(x - 2)^2(x - 5) = x^3 - 9x^2 + 24x - 20$.

    (ii) Hence sketch the graph of $y = x^3 - 9x^2 + 24x - 20$.　　4

23. The diagram shows a sketch of functions f and g where $f(x) = x^3 + 5x^2 - 36x + 32$ and $g(x) = -x^2 + x + 2$.

    The two graphs intersect at the points A, B and C.

    Determine the x-coordinate of each of these three points.　　8

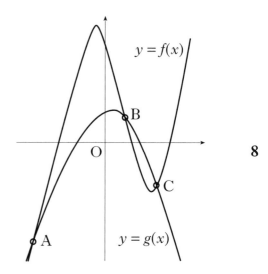

24. Find the solution(s) of the equation $\sin^2 p - \sin p + 1 = \cos^2 p$ for $\frac{\pi}{2} < p < \pi$.　　5

[END OF SECTION B]

[END OF QUESTION PAPER]

[C100/SQP321]

Mathematics

Higher

Paper 2

Specimen Question Paper

(for examinations from Diet 2008 onwards)

NATIONAL
QUALIFICATIONS

Read Carefully

1   **Calculators may be used in this paper.**

2   Full credit will be given only where the solution contains appropriate working.

3   Answers obtained by readings from scale drawings will not receive any credit.

SCOTTISH
QUALIFICATIONS
AUTHORITY
©

FORMULAE LIST

Circle:

The equation $x^2 + y^2 + 2gx + 2fy + c = 0$ represents a circle centre $(-g, -f)$ and radius $\sqrt{g^2 + f^2 - c}$.

The equation $(x - a)^2 + (y - b)^2 = r^2$ represents a circle centre (a, b) and radius r.

Scalar Product: $a.b = |a|\,|b|\cos\theta$, where θ is the angle between a and b

or $a.b = a_1b_1 + a_2b_2 + a_3b_3$ where $a = \begin{pmatrix} a_1 \\ a_2 \\ a_3 \end{pmatrix}$ and $b = \begin{pmatrix} b_1 \\ b_2 \\ b_3 \end{pmatrix}$.

Trigonometric formulae:
$$\sin(A \pm B) = \sin A \cos B \pm \cos A \sin B$$
$$\cos(A \pm B) = \cos A \cos B \mp \sin A \sin B$$
$$\sin 2A = 2\sin A \cos A$$
$$\cos 2A = \cos^2 A - \sin^2 A$$
$$= 2\cos^2 A - 1$$
$$= 1 - 2\sin^2 A$$

Table of standard derivatives:

$f(x)$	$f'(x)$
$\sin ax$	$a\cos ax$
$\cos ax$	$-a\sin ax$

Table of standard integrals:

$f(x)$	$\int f(x)\,dx$
$\sin ax$	$-\dfrac{1}{a}\cos ax + C$
$\cos ax$	$\dfrac{1}{a}\sin ax + C$

ALL questions should be attempted.

Marks

1. Triangle ABC has coordinates A(2, 1), B(10, 1) and C(4, 7).

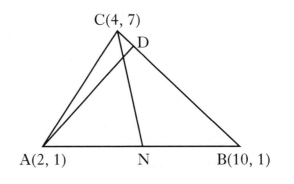

   (a) Find the equation of the median CN.   **3**

   (b) Find the equation of the altitude AD.   **3**

   (c) The median from (a) and the altitude from (b) intersect at P. Find the coordinates of P.   **3**

   (d) The point Q lies on AB and has coordinates (8, 1).

   Show that PQ is parallel to BC.   **2**

2. The diagram shows a wire framework in the shape of a cuboid with the edges parallel to the axes.

   Relative to these axes, A, B, C and H have coordinates (1, 3, 4), (2, 3, 4), (2, 7, 4) and (1, 7, 9) respectively.

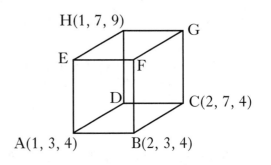

   (a) State the lengths of AB, AD and AE.   **1**

   (b) Write down the components of $\overrightarrow{HB}$ and $\overrightarrow{HC}$ and hence or otherwise calculate the size of angle BHC.   **7**

3. (a) Express $5\sin x° - 12\cos x°$ in the form $k\sin(x - a)°$ where $k > 0$ and $0 < a < 360$.   **4**

   (b) Hence solve the equation $5\sin x° - 12\cos x° = 6·5$ in the interval $0 < x < 360$.   **3**

Marks

4. The diagram shows a parabola with equation $y = 2x^2 - 2x + 3$.

   A tangent to the parabola has been drawn at P(1, 3).

   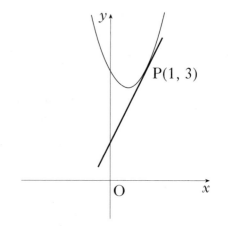

   (a) Find the equation of this tangent. **4**

   A circle has equation $x^2 + y^2 + 8y + 11 = 0$.

   (b) Show that the line from (a) is also a tangent to this circle and state the coordinates of the point of contact Q. **6**

   (c) Determine the ratio in which the y-axis cuts the line QP. **3**

5. The diagram shows a curve with equation $y = x^2$ and a straight line with equation $y = 6x + 16$ intersecting the curve at P and Q.

   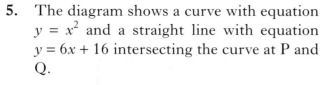

   (a) Calculate the exact value of the area enclosed by the curve and the straight line. **7**

   The second diagram shows a third point, R, lying on the curve between P and Q.

   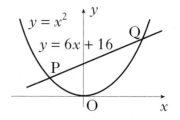

   (b) The area, A, of triangle PQR, is given by $A(x) = -5x^2 + 30x + 80$.

   Determine the maximum area of this triangle, and express your answer as a fraction of the area enclosed by the curve and the straight line. **4**

6. Radium decays exponentially and its half-life is 1600 years.

   If A_0 represents the amount of radium in a sample to start with and $A(t)$ represents the amount remaining after t years, then $A(t) = A_0 e^{-kt}$.

   (a) Determine the value of k, correct to 4 significant figures. **3**

   (b) Hence find what percentage, to the nearest whole number, of the original amount of radium will be remaining after 3200 years. **2**

Marks

7. Triangle ABC is right-angled at A and BD is the bisector of angle ABC.

   AB = 6 units and CB = 10 units.

   Determine the exact value of BD, expressing your answer in its simplest form.

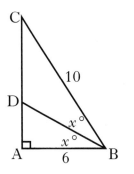

5

[END OF QUESTION PAPER]

[BLANK PAGE]

HIGHER

2008

[BLANK PAGE]

X100/301

NATIONAL QUALIFICATIONS 2008	TUESDAY, 20 MAY 9.00 AM – 10.30 AM	MATHEMATICS HIGHER Paper 1 (Non-calculator)

Read carefully

Calculators may <u>NOT</u> be used in this paper.

Section A – Questions 1–20 (40 marks)

Instructions for completion of **Section A** are given on page two.

For this section of the examination you must use an **HB pencil**.

Section B (30 marks)

1   Full credit will be given only where the solution contains appropriate working.

2   Answers obtained by readings from scale drawings will not receive any credit.

Read carefully

1 Check that the answer sheet provided is for **Mathematics Higher (Section A)**.

2 For this section of the examination you must use an **HB pencil** and, where necessary, an eraser.

3 Check that the answer sheet you have been given has **your name**, **date of birth**, **SCN** (Scottish Candidate Number) and **Centre Name** printed on it.

    Do not change any of these details.

4 If any of this information is wrong, tell the Invigilator immediately.

5 If this information is correct, **print** your name and seat number in the boxes provided.

6 The answer to each question is **either** A, B, C or D. Decide what your answer is, then, using your pencil, put a horizontal line in the space provided (see sample question below).

7 There is **only one correct** answer to each question.

8 Rough working should **not** be done on your answer sheet.

9 At the end of the exam, put the **answer sheet for Section A inside the front cover of your answer book**.

Sample Question

A curve has equation $y = x^3 - 4x$.

What is the gradient at the point where $x = 2$?

    A   8

    B   1

    C   0

    D   −4

The correct answer is **A**—8. The answer **A** has been clearly marked in **pencil** with a horizontal line (see below).

A   B   C   D

Changing an answer

If you decide to change your answer, carefully erase your first answer and using your pencil, fill in the answer you want. The answer below has been changed to **D**.

A   B   C   D

FORMULAE LIST

Circle:

The equation $x^2 + y^2 + 2gx + 2fy + c = 0$ represents a circle centre $(-g, -f)$ and radius $\sqrt{g^2 + f^2 - c}$.

The equation $(x - a)^2 + (y - b)^2 = r^2$ represents a circle centre (a, b) and radius r.

Scalar Product: $a.b = |a|\,|b| \cos \theta$, where θ is the angle between a and b

or $a.b = a_1b_1 + a_2b_2 + a_3b_3$ where $a = \begin{pmatrix} a_1 \\ a_2 \\ a_3 \end{pmatrix}$ and $b = \begin{pmatrix} b_1 \\ b_2 \\ b_3 \end{pmatrix}$.

Trigonometric formulae:

$$\sin (A \pm B) = \sin A \cos B \pm \cos A \sin B$$
$$\cos (A \pm B) = \cos A \cos B \mp \sin A \sin B$$
$$\sin 2A = 2\sin A \cos A$$
$$\cos 2A = \cos^2 A - \sin^2 A$$
$$= 2\cos^2 A - 1$$
$$= 1 - 2\sin^2 A$$

Table of standard derivatives:

$f(x)$	$f'(x)$
$\sin ax$	$a \cos ax$
$\cos ax$	$-a \sin ax$

Table of standard integrals:

$f(x)$	$\int f(x)\,dx$
$\sin ax$	$-\dfrac{1}{a} \cos ax + C$
$\cos ax$	$\dfrac{1}{a} \sin ax + C$

[Turn over

SECTION A

ALL questions should be attempted.

1. A sequence is defined by the recurrence relation

   $$u_{n+1} = 0 \cdot 3u_n + 6 \text{ with } u_{10} = 10.$$

   What is the value of u_{12}?

   A   6·6

   B   7·8

   C   8·7

   D   9·6

2. The x-axis is a tangent to a circle with centre $(-7, 6)$ as shown in the diagram.

   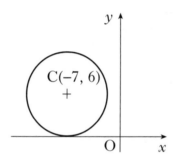

   What is the equation of the circle?

   A $(x + 7)^2 + (y - 6)^2 = 1$

   B $(x + 7)^2 + (y - 6)^2 = 49$

   C $(x - 7)^2 + (y + 6)^2 = 36$

   D $(x + 7)^2 + (y - 6)^2 = 36$

3. The vectors $\boldsymbol{u} = \begin{pmatrix} k \\ -1 \\ 1 \end{pmatrix}$ and $\boldsymbol{v} = \begin{pmatrix} 0 \\ 4 \\ k \end{pmatrix}$ are perpendicular.

   What is the value of k?

   A   0

   B   3

   C   4

   D   5

4. A sequence is generated by the recurrence relation $u_{n+1} = 0\cdot4u_n - 240$.

   What is the limit of this sequence as $n \to \infty$?

   A -800

   B -400

   C 200

   D 400

5. The diagram shows a circle, centre (2, 5) and a tangent drawn at the point (7, 9).

   What is the equation of this tangent?

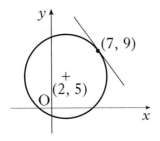

   A $y - 9 = -\dfrac{5}{4}(x - 7)$

   B $y + 9 = -\dfrac{4}{5}(x + 7)$

   C $y - 7 = \dfrac{4}{5}(x - 9)$

   D $y + 9 = \dfrac{5}{4}(x + 7)$

[Turn over

6. What is the solution of the equation $2\sin x - \sqrt{3} = 0$ where $\frac{\pi}{2} \leq x \leq \pi$?

A $\quad \dfrac{\pi}{6}$

B $\quad \dfrac{2\pi}{3}$

C $\quad \dfrac{3\pi}{4}$

D $\quad \dfrac{5\pi}{6}$

7. The diagram shows a line L; the angle between L and the positive direction of the x-axis is 135°, as shown.

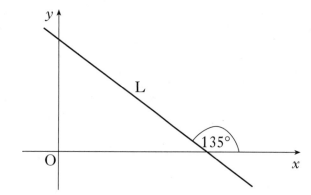

What is the gradient of line L?

A $\quad -\dfrac{1}{2}$

B $\quad -\dfrac{\sqrt{3}}{2}$

C $\quad -1$

D $\quad \dfrac{1}{2}$

8. The diagram shows part of the graph of a function with equation $y = f(x)$.

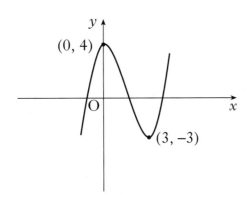

Which of the following diagrams shows the graph with equation $y = -f(x - 2)$?

A

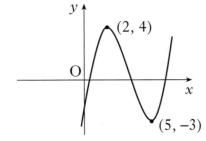

B

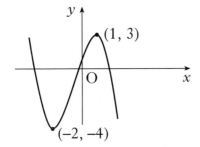

C

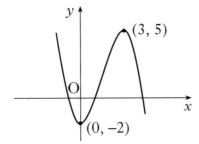

D

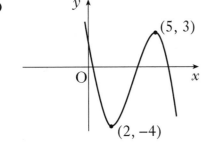

9. Given that $0 \le a \le \frac{\pi}{2}$ and $\sin a = \frac{3}{5}$, find an expression for $\sin(x + a)$.

A $\sin x + \frac{3}{5}$

B $\frac{4}{5}\sin x + \frac{3}{5}\cos x$

C $\frac{3}{5}\sin x - \frac{4}{5}\cos x$

D $\frac{2}{5}\sin x - \frac{3}{5}\cos x$

10. Here are two statements about the roots of the equation $x^2 + x + 1 = 0$:

(1) the roots are equal;

(2) the roots are real.

Which of the following is true?

A Neither statement is correct.

B Only statement (1) is correct.

C Only statement (2) is correct.

D Both statements are correct.

11. E(−2, −1, 4), P(1, 5, 7) and F(7, 17, 13) are three collinear points.

P lies between E and F.

What is the ratio in which P divides EF?

A 1:1

B 1:2

C 1:4

D 1:6

12. In the diagram RSTU, VWXY represents a cuboid.

$\overrightarrow{SR}$ represents vector f, $\overrightarrow{ST}$ represents vector g and $\overrightarrow{SW}$ represents vector h.

Express $\overrightarrow{VT}$ in terms of f, g and h.

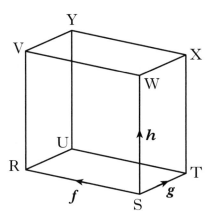

A $\overrightarrow{VT} = f + g + h$

B $\overrightarrow{VT} = f - g + h$

C $\overrightarrow{VT} = -f + g - h$

D $\overrightarrow{VT} = -f - g + h$

13. The diagram shows part of the graph of a quadratic function $y = f(x)$.

The graph has an equation of the form $y = k(x - a)(x - b)$.

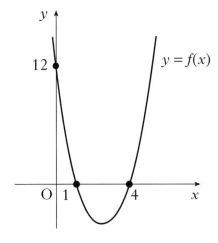

What is the equation of the graph?

A $y = 3(x - 1)(x - 4)$

B $y = 3(x + 1)(x + 4)$

C $y = 12(x - 1)(x - 4)$

D $y = 12(x + 1)(x + 4)$

14. Find $\int 4\sin(2x+3)\,dx$.

A　$-4\cos(2x+3)+c$

B　$-2\cos(2x+3)+c$

C　$4\cos(2x+3)+c$

D　$8\cos(2x+3)+c$

15. What is the derivative of $(x^3+4)^2$?

A　$(3x^2+4)^2$

B　$\dfrac{1}{3}(x^3+4)^3$

C　$6x^2(x^3+4)$

D　$2(3x^2+4)^{-1}$

16. $2x^2+4x+7$ is expressed in the form $2(x+p)^2+q$.

What is the value of q?

A　5

B　7

C　9

D　11

17. A function f is given by $f(x)=\sqrt{9-x^2}$.

What is a suitable domain of f?

A　$x\geq 3$

B　$x\leq 3$

C　$-3\leq x\leq 3$

D　$-9\leq x\leq 9$

18. Vectors $\boldsymbol{p}$ and $\boldsymbol{q}$ are such that $|\boldsymbol{p}| = 3$, $|\boldsymbol{q}| = 4$ and $\boldsymbol{p}.\boldsymbol{q} = 10$.

Find the value of $\boldsymbol{q}.(\boldsymbol{p} + \boldsymbol{q})$.

A   0

B   14

C   26

D   28

19. The diagram shows part of the graph whose equation is of the form $y = 2m^x$.

What is the value of m?

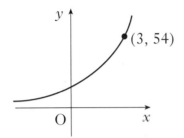

A   2

B   3

C   8

D   18

20. The diagram shows part of the graph of $y = \log_3(x - 4)$.

The point $(q, 2)$ lies on the graph.

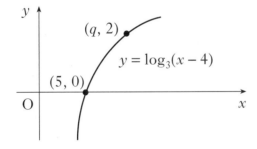

What is the value of q?

A   6

B   7

C   8

D   13

[END OF SECTION A]

SECTION B

ALL questions should be attempted.

Marks

21. A function f is defined on the set of real numbers by $f(x) = x^3 - 3x + 2$.

    (a) Find the coordinates of the stationary points on the curve $y = f(x)$ and determine their nature.   **6**

    (b) (i) Show that $(x - 1)$ is a factor of $x^3 - 3x + 2$.

       (ii) Hence or otherwise factorise $x^3 - 3x + 2$ fully.   **5**

    (c) State the coordinates of the points where the curve with equation $y = f(x)$ meets both the axes and hence sketch the curve.   **4**

22. The diagram shows a sketch of the curve with equation $y = x^3 - 6x^2 + 8x$.

    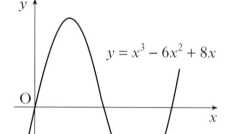

    (a) Find the coordinates of the points on the curve where the gradient of the tangent is -1.   **5**

    (b) The line $y = 4 - x$ is a tangent to this curve at a point A. Find the coordinates of A.   **2**

23. Functions f, g and h are defined on suitable domains by

    $$f(x) = x^2 - x + 10,\ g(x) = 5 - x \text{ and } h(x) = \log_2 x.$$

    (a) Find expressions for $h(f(x))$ and $h(g(x))$.   **3**

    (b) Hence solve $h(f(x)) - h(g(x)) = 3$.   **5**

[END OF SECTION B]

[END OF QUESTION PAPER]

X100/302

NATIONAL
QUALIFICATIONS
2008

TUESDAY, 20 MAY
10.50 AM – 12.00 NOON

MATHEMATICS
HIGHER
Paper 2

Read Carefully

1 **Calculators may be used in this paper.**

2 Full credit will be given only where the solution contains appropriate working.

3 Answers obtained by readings from scale drawings will not receive any credit.

✕SQA

FORMULAE LIST

Circle:

The equation $x^2 + y^2 + 2gx + 2fy + c = 0$ represents a circle centre $(-g, -f)$ and radius $\sqrt{g^2 + f^2 - c}$.

The equation $(x - a)^2 + (y - b)^2 = r^2$ represents a circle centre (a, b) and radius r.

Scalar Product: $a.b = |a|\,|b| \cos \theta$, where θ is the angle between a and b

or $a.b = a_1 b_1 + a_2 b_2 + a_3 b_3$ where $a = \begin{pmatrix} a_1 \\ a_2 \\ a_3 \end{pmatrix}$ and $b = \begin{pmatrix} b_1 \\ b_2 \\ b_3 \end{pmatrix}$.

Trigonometric formulae:

$$\sin (A \pm B) = \sin A \cos B \pm \cos A \sin B$$
$$\cos (A \pm B) = \cos A \cos B \mp \sin A \sin B$$
$$\sin 2A = 2\sin A \cos A$$
$$\cos 2A = \cos^2 A - \sin^2 A$$
$$= 2\cos^2 A - 1$$
$$= 1 - 2\sin^2 A$$

Table of standard derivatives:

$f(x)$	$f'(x)$
$\sin ax$	$a \cos ax$
$\cos ax$	$-a \sin ax$

Table of standard integrals:

$f(x)$	$\int f(x)\,dx$
$\sin ax$	$-\dfrac{1}{a}\cos ax + C$
$\cos ax$	$\dfrac{1}{a}\sin ax + C$

ALL questions should be attempted.

Marks

1. The vertices of triangle ABC are A(7, 9), B(−3, −1) and C(5, −5) as shown in the diagram.

    The broken line represents the perpendicular bisector of BC.

    (a) Show that the equation of the perpendicular bisector of BC is $y = 2x - 5$.

    4

    (b) Find the equation of the median from C.

    3

    (c) Find the coordinates of the point of intersection of the perpendicular bisector of BC and the median from C.

    3

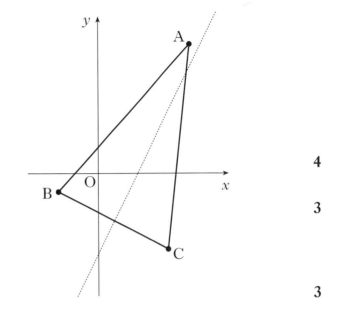

2. The diagram shows a cuboid OABC, DEFG.

    F is the point (8, 4, 6).

    P divides AE in the ratio 2:1.

    Q is the midpoint of CG.

    (a) State the coordinates of P and Q.

    2

    (b) Write down the components of $\overrightarrow{PQ}$ and $\overrightarrow{PA}$.

    2

    (c) Find the size of angle QPA.

    5

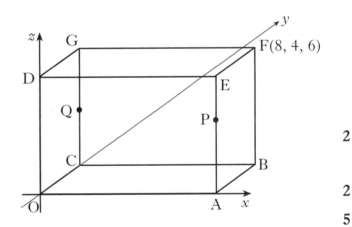

[Turn over

Marks

3. (*a*) (i) Diagram 1 shows part of the
   graph of $y = f(x)$, where
   $f(x) = p\cos x$.

   Write down the value of p.   Diagram 1

   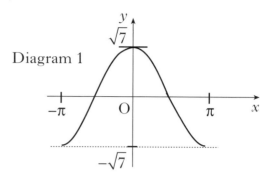

   (ii) Diagram 2 shows part of the
   graph of $y = g(x)$, where
   $g(x) = q\sin x$.

   Write down the value of q.   Diagram 2   **2**

   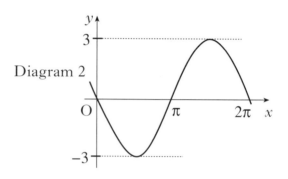

   (*b*) Write $f(x) + g(x)$ in the form $k\cos(x + a)$ where $k > 0$ and $0 < a < \dfrac{\pi}{2}$.   **4**

   (*c*) Hence find $f'(x) + g'(x)$ as a single trigonometric expression.   **2**

4. (*a*) Write down the centre and calculate the radius of the circle with equation
   $x^2 + y^2 + 8x + 4y - 38 = 0$.   **2**

   (*b*) A second circle has equation $(x - 4)^2 + (y - 6)^2 = 26$.

   Find the distance between the centres of these two circles and hence show
   that the circles intersect.   **4**

   (*c*) The line with equation $y = 4 - x$ is a common chord passing through the
   points of intersection of the two circles.

   Find the coordinates of the points of intersection of the two circles.   **5**

5. Solve the equation $\cos 2x° + 2\sin x° = \sin^2 x°$ in the interval $0 \le x < 360$.   **5**

Marks

6. In the diagram, Q lies on the line joining (0, 6) and (3, 0).

    OPQR is a rectangle, where P and R lie on the axes and OR = t.

    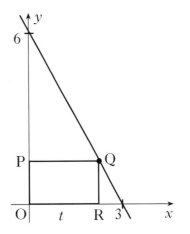

    (a) Show that QR = $6 - 2t$.   **3**

    (b) Find the coordinates of Q for which the rectangle has a maximum area.   **6**

7. The parabola shown in the diagram has equation

    $y = 32 - 2x^2$.

    The shaded area lies between the lines $y = 14$ and $y = 24$.

    Calculate the shaded area.   **8**

    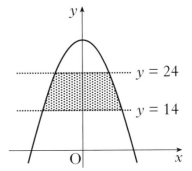

[*END OF QUESTION PAPER*]

[BLANK PAGE]

[BLANK PAGE]

[C100/SQP328]

Mathematics

Higher

Paper 1

Specimen Question Paper

Example 2 based on 2004 Examination Paper

(for examinations from Diet 2008 onwards)

NATIONAL

QUALIFICATIONS

Read carefully

Calculators may NOT be used in this paper.

Section A – Questions 1–20 (40 marks)

Instructions for completion of **Section A** are given on page two.

For this section of the examination you must use an **HB pencil**.

Section B (30 marks)

1   Full credit will be given only where the solution contains appropriate working.

2   Answers obtained by readings from scale drawings will not receive any credit.

Read carefully

1   Check that the answer sheet provided is for **Mathematics Higher (Section A)**.

2   For this section of the examination you must use an **HB pencil** and, where necessary, an eraser.

3   Check that the answer sheet you have been given has **your name**, **date of birth**, **SCN** (Scottish Candidate Number) and **Centre Name** printed on it.

    Do not change any of these details.

4   If any of this information is wrong, tell the Invigilator immediately.

5   If this information is correct, **print** your name and seat number in the boxes provided.

6   The answer to each question is **either** A, B, C or D. Decide what your answer is, then, using your pencil, put a horizontal line in the space provided (see sample question below).

7   There is **only one correct** answer to each question.

8   Rough working should **not** be done on your answer sheet.

9   At the end of the exam, put the **answer sheet for Section A inside the front cover of your answer book**.

Sample Question

A curve has equation $y = x^3 - 4x$.

What is the gradient at the point where $x = 2$?

    A   8

    B   1

    C   0

    D −4

The correct answer is **A**—8. The answer **A** has been clearly marked in **pencil** with a horizontal line (see below).

Changing an answer

If you decide to change your answer, carefully erase your first answer and using your pencil, fill in the answer you want. The answer below has been changed to **D**.

FORMULAE LIST

Circle:

The equation $x^2 + y^2 + 2gx + 2fy + c = 0$ represents a circle centre $(-g, -f)$ and radius $\sqrt{g^2 + f^2 - c}$.

The equation $(x - a)^2 + (y - b)^2 = r^2$ represents a circle centre (a, b) and radius r.

Scalar Product: $a.b = |a|\,|b| \cos \theta$, where θ is the angle between a and b

or $a.b = a_1b_1 + a_2b_2 + a_3b_3$ where $a = \begin{pmatrix} a_1 \\ a_2 \\ a_3 \end{pmatrix}$ and $b = \begin{pmatrix} b_1 \\ b_2 \\ b_3 \end{pmatrix}$.

Trigonometric formulae:
$$\sin (A \pm B) = \sin A \cos B \pm \cos A \sin B$$
$$\cos (A \pm B) = \cos A \cos B \mp \sin A \sin B$$
$$\sin 2A = 2\sin A \cos A$$
$$\cos 2A = \cos^2 A - \sin^2 A$$
$$= 2\cos^2 A - 1$$
$$= 1 - 2\sin^2 A$$

Table of standard derivatives:

$f(x)$	$f'(x)$
$\sin ax$	$a \cos ax$
$\cos ax$	$-a \sin ax$

Table of standard integrals:

$f(x)$	$\int f(x)\,dx$
$\sin ax$	$-\dfrac{1}{a} \cos ax + C$
$\cos ax$	$\dfrac{1}{a} \sin ax + C$

SECTION A

ALL questions should be attempted.

1. The line through P(7, p) and Q(4, −5) has a gradient of 3.

   What is the value of p?

   A   −14

   B   4

   C   6

   D   8

2. A sequence is defined by the recurrence relation $u_{n+1} = u_n + 5$, $u_0 = -3$.

   What is the value of u_2?

   A   3
   B   5
   C   7
   D   9

3. What is the gradient of the line perpendicular to the line with equation $3y = -2x + 1$?

   A   −3

   B   1

   C $\dfrac{3}{2}$

   D   5

4. $f(x) = x^3 - x^2 - 5x - 3$.

   What is the remainder when $f(x)$ is divided by $(x + 3)$?

   A   −24
   B   −3
   C   36
   D   48

5. If $x^2 - 16x + 27$ is written in the form $(x + p)^2 + q$, find the value of q.

   A -37

   B 11

   C 27

   D 43

6. What is the derivative of $(8 - 2x^2)^{\frac{2}{3}}$?

   A $-\dfrac{8}{3}x(8 - 2x^2)^{-\frac{1}{3}}$

   B $(8 - 4x)^{\frac{2}{3}}$

   C $\dfrac{2}{3}(8 - 4x)^{-\frac{1}{3}}$

   D $\dfrac{3}{5}(8 - 2x^2)^{\frac{5}{3}}$

7. On dividing $f(x)$ by $(x - 1)$, the remainder is zero and the quotient is $x^2 - 4x - 5$. Find $f(x)$ in its fully factorised form.

   A $(x - 1)(x - 1)(x + 5)$

   B $(x + 1)(x - 5)$

   C $(x - 1)(x - 1)$

   D $(x - 1)(x + 1)(x - 5)$

8. A sequence is generated by the recurrence relation $u_{n+1} = 0{\cdot}4u_n + 3$. What is the limit of this sequence as $n \to \infty$?

   A $\dfrac{1}{5}$

   B $\dfrac{15}{7}$

   C 5

   D $\dfrac{15}{2}$

9. Find all the values of x in the interval $0 < x < 2\pi$ for which $\tan x = -\sqrt{3}$.

A $\dfrac{5\pi}{6}, \dfrac{11\pi}{6}$

B $\dfrac{2\pi}{3}, \dfrac{4\pi}{3}$

C $\dfrac{2\pi}{3}, \dfrac{5\pi}{3}$

D $\dfrac{5\pi}{3}, \dfrac{7\pi}{3}$

10. $P = (-3, 4, 7)$, $Q = (-1, 8, 3)$ and $R = (0, 10, 1)$.

Find the ratio in which Q divides PR.

A $2 : 1$

B $3 : -1$

C $1 : 2$

D $3 : 1$

11. The diagram shows the line OP with equation $2y = x$.

The angle between OP and the positive direction of the x-axis is $p°$.

Find an expression for angle p.

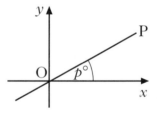

A $\tan^{-1}\frac{1}{2}$

B $\tan^{-1}1$

C $\tan^{-1}2$

D $-\tan^{-1}\frac{1}{2}$

12. Which one of the following is true for the function g where $g'(x) = x^2 + 2x + 1$?

    A g is never increasing.

    B g is decreasing then increasing.

    C g is increasing then decreasing.

    D g is never decreasing.

13. Simplify $\log_2(x + 1) - 2\log_2 3$.

    A $\log_2\left(\dfrac{x+1}{9}\right)$

    B $\log_2(x - 8)$

    C $\log_2(x - 2)$

    D $\log_2 6(x + 1)$

14. The diagram shows the graph of $y = g(x)$.

Which diagram below shows the graph of $y = 3 - g(x)$?

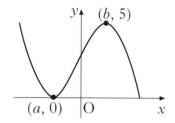

A

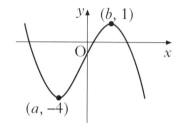

B

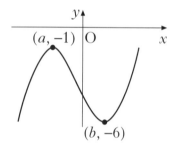

C

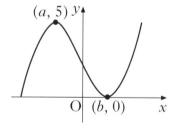

D

15. Points P and Q have coordinates $(1, 3, -1)$ and $(2, 5, 1)$ and T is the midpoint of PQ.

What is the position vector of T?

A $\begin{pmatrix} -\dfrac{3}{2} \\ -4 \\ 0 \end{pmatrix}$

B $\begin{pmatrix} \dfrac{3}{2} \\ 4 \\ 0 \end{pmatrix}$

C $\begin{pmatrix} -\dfrac{1}{2} \\ -1 \\ -1 \end{pmatrix}$

D $\begin{pmatrix} -1 \\ -2 \\ -2 \end{pmatrix}$

16. $A = (-3, 4, 7)$ and $B = (-1, 8, 3)$.

If $\overrightarrow{AD} = 4\overrightarrow{AB}$, what are the coordinates of D?

A $(-9, -8, -13)$

B $(5, -4, 1)$

C $(-6, 8, 14)$

D $(5, 20, -9)$

17. The equation of the parabola shown is of the form $y = kx(x - 6)$.

What is the value of k?

A   0

B $\dfrac{1}{144}$

C   2

D   6

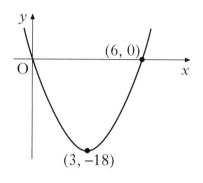

18. Given that $y = 3\cos 5x$, find $\dfrac{dy}{dx}$.

A $15\cos 5x$

B $-15\sin 5x$

C $-15\cos x$

D $3\cos 5$

19. Find $\displaystyle\int (4x+1)^{\frac{1}{2}} \, dx$.

A $\dfrac{1}{6}(4x+1)^{\frac{3}{2}} + c$

B $\dfrac{1}{4}(4x+1) + c$

C $\dfrac{1}{4}(4x+1)^{\frac{3}{2}} + c$

D $2(4x+1)^{-\frac{3}{2}} + c$

20. Given that $\int (3x+1)^{-\frac{1}{2}} \, dx = \frac{2}{3}(3x+1)^{\frac{1}{2}} + c,$ find $\int_{0}^{1}(3x+1)^{-\frac{1}{2}} \, dx.$

A $\quad \frac{2}{3}$

B $\quad \frac{4}{3}$

C $\quad 2$

D $\quad \sqrt{2}$

[END OF SECTION A]

SECTION B

ALL questions should be attempted.

Marks

21. (*a*) Find the stationary points on the curve with equation $y = x^3 + 3x^2 - 9x + 5$ and justify their nature.　　**7**

    (*b*) The curve passes through the point (−5, 0). Sketch the curve.　　**2**

22. Solve the equation $\log_x 8 + \log_x 4 = 5$.　　**4**

23. Solve the equation $\sin 2x - \cos x = 0$ for $0 \le x \le 2\pi$.　　**5**

24. In the diagram,

    angle DEC = angle CEB = $x°$ and
    angle CDE = angle BEA = $90°$.
    CD = 1 unit; DE = 3 units.

    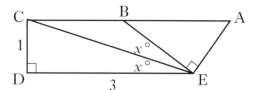

    By writing angle DEA in terms of $x°$,
    find the exact value of $\cos(\hat{DEA})$.　　**7**

25. The diagram shows a parabola with equation

    $$y = 6x(x - 2).$$

    This parabola is the graph of $y = f'(x)$.

    Given that $f(1) = 4$, find the formula for $f(x)$.　　**5**

    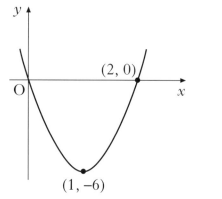

[*END OF SECTION B*]

[*END OF QUESTION PAPER*]

[C100/SQP328]

Mathematics
Higher
Paper 2
Specimen Question Paper
Example 2 based on 2004 Examination Paper
(for examinations from Diet 2008 onwards)

NATIONAL
QUALIFICATIONS

Read Carefully

1   **Calculators may be used in this paper.**

2   Full credit will be given only where the solution contains appropriate working.

3   Answers obtained by readings from scale drawings will not receive any credit.

FORMULAE LIST

Circle:

The equation $x^2 + y^2 + 2gx + 2fy + c = 0$ represents a circle centre $(-g, -f)$ and radius $\sqrt{g^2 + f^2 - c}$.

The equation $(x - a)^2 + (y - b)^2 = r^2$ represents a circle centre (a, b) and radius r.

Scalar Product: $\quad a.b = |a|\,|b| \cos \theta$, where θ is the angle between a and b

$\qquad$ or $\quad a.b = a_1b_1 + a_2b_2 + a_3b_3$ where $a = \begin{pmatrix} a_1 \\ a_2 \\ a_3 \end{pmatrix}$ and $b = \begin{pmatrix} b_1 \\ b_2 \\ b_3 \end{pmatrix}$.

Trigonometric formulae:
$$\sin (A \pm B) = \sin A \cos B \pm \cos A \sin B$$
$$\cos (A \pm B) = \cos A \cos B \mp \sin A \sin B$$
$$\sin 2A = 2\sin A \cos A$$
$$\cos 2A = \cos^2 A - \sin^2 A$$
$$= 2\cos^2 A - 1$$
$$= 1 - 2\sin^2 A$$

Table of standard derivatives:

$f(x)$	$f'(x)$
$\sin ax$	$a \cos ax$
$\cos ax$	$-a \sin ax$

Table of standard integrals:

$f(x)$	$\int f(x)\,dx$
$\sin ax$	$-\dfrac{1}{a} \cos ax + C$
$\cos ax$	$\dfrac{1}{a} \sin ax + C$

ALL questions should be attempted.

Marks

1. Given that $\overrightarrow{QP} = \begin{pmatrix} -1 \\ 3 \\ -2 \end{pmatrix}$ and $\overrightarrow{QR} = \begin{pmatrix} -5 \\ 1 \\ 1 \end{pmatrix}$, find the size of angle PQR. **5**

2. Prove that the roots of the equation $2x^2 + px - 3 = 0$ are real for all values of p. **4**

3. The point $P(x, y)$ lies on the curve with equation $y = 6x^2 - x^3$.

    (a) Find the value of x for which the gradient of the tangent at P is 12. **5**

    (b) Hence find the equation of the tangent at P. **2**

4. (a) Express $3\cos x° + 5\sin x°$ in the form $k\cos(x° - a°)$ where $k > 0$ and $0 \le a \le 90$. **4**

    (b) Hence solve the equation $3\cos x° + 5\sin x° = 4$ for $0 \le x \le 90$. **3**

5. The graph of the cubic function $y = f(x)$ is shown in the diagram. There are turning points at $(1, 1)$ and $(3, 5)$.

    Sketch the graph of $y = f'(x)$. **3**

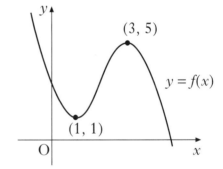

Marks

6. The circle with centre A has equation $x^2 + y^2 - 12x - 2y + 32 = 0$. The line PT is a tangent to this circle at the point P(5, –1).

    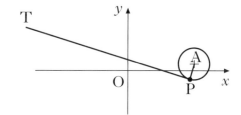

    (a) Show that the equation of this tangent is $x + 2y = 3$.   **4**

    The circle with centre B has equation $x^2 + y^2 + 10x + 2y + 6 = 0$.

    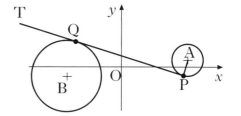

    (b) Show that PT is also a tangent to this circle.   **5**

    (c) Q is the point of contact. Find the length of PQ.   **2**

7. An open cuboid measures internally x units by $2x$ units by h units and has an inner surface area of 12 units^2.

    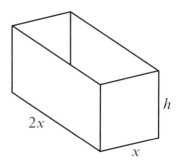

    (a) Show that the volume, V units^3, of the cuboid is given by $V(x) = \frac{2}{3}x(6 - x^2)$.   **3**

    (b) Find the exact value of x for which this volume is a maximum.   **5**

8. The amount A_t micrograms of a certain radioactive substance remaining after t years decreases according to the formula $A_t = A_0 e^{-0.002t}$, where A_0 is the amount present initially.

    (a) If 600 micrograms are left after 1000 years, how many micrograms were present initially?   **3**

    (b) The half-life of a substance is the time taken for the amount to decrease to half of its initial amount. What is the half-life of this substance?   **4**

Marks

9. An architectural feature of a building is a wall with arched windows. The curved edge of each window is parabolic.

    The second diagram shows one such window. The shaded part represents the glass.

    The top edge of the window is part of the parabola with equation $y = 2x - \frac{1}{2}x^2$.

    Find the area in square metres of the glass in one window.

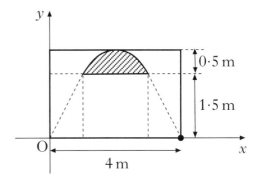

8

[END OF QUESTION PAPER]

[BLANK PAGE]

2009

[BLANK PAGE]

X100/301

NATIONAL
QUALIFICATIONS
2009

THURSDAY, 21 MAY
9.00 AM – 10.30 AM

MATHEMATICS
HIGHER
Paper 1
(Non-calculator)

Read carefully

Calculators may <u>NOT</u> be used in this paper.

Section A — Questions 1—20 (40 marks)

Instructions for completion of **Section A** are given on page two.

For this section of the examination you must use an **HB pencil**.

Section B (30 marks)

1   Full credit will be given only where the solution contains appropriate working.

2   Answers obtained by readings from scale drawings will not receive any credit.

Read carefully

1 Check that the answer sheet provided is for **Mathematics Higher (Section A)**.

2 For this section of the examination you must use an **HB pencil** and, where necessary, an eraser.

3 Check that the answer sheet you have been given has **your name**, **date of birth**, **SCN** (Scottish Candidate Number) and **Centre Name** printed on it.

   Do not change any of these details.

4 If any of this information is wrong, tell the Invigilator immediately.

5 If this information is correct, **print** your name and seat number in the boxes provided.

6 The answer to each question is **either** A, B, C or D. Decide what your answer is, then, using your pencil, put a horizontal line in the space provided (see sample question below).

7 There is **only one correct** answer to each question.

8 Rough working should **not** be done on your answer sheet.

9 At the end of the exam, put the **answer sheet for Section A inside the front cover of your answer book**.

Sample Question

A curve has equation $y = x^3 - 4x$.

What is the gradient at the point where $x = 2$?

   A   8

   B   1

   C   0

   D −4

The correct answer is **A**—8. The answer **A** has been clearly marked in **pencil** with a horizontal line (see below).

Changing an answer

If you decide to change your answer, carefully erase your first answer and, using your pencil, fill in the answer you want. The answer below has been changed to **D**.

FORMULAE LIST

Circle:

The equation $x^2 + y^2 + 2gx + 2fy + c = 0$ represents a circle centre $(-g, -f)$ and radius $\sqrt{g^2 + f^2 - c}$.

The equation $(x - a)^2 + (y - b)^2 = r^2$ represents a circle centre (a, b) and radius r.

Scalar Product: $\quad \boldsymbol{a.b} = |\boldsymbol{a}|\,|\boldsymbol{b}| \cos \theta$, where θ is the angle between $\boldsymbol{a}$ and $\boldsymbol{b}$

or $\quad \boldsymbol{a.b} = a_1 b_1 + a_2 b_2 + a_3 b_3$ where $\boldsymbol{a} = \begin{pmatrix} a_1 \\ a_2 \\ a_3 \end{pmatrix}$ and $\boldsymbol{b} = \begin{pmatrix} b_1 \\ b_2 \\ b_3 \end{pmatrix}$.

Trigonometric formulae:

$$\sin (A \pm B) = \sin A \cos B \pm \cos A \sin B$$
$$\cos (A \pm B) = \cos A \cos B \mp \sin A \sin B$$
$$\sin 2A = 2\sin A \cos A$$
$$\cos 2A = \cos^2 A - \sin^2 A$$
$$= 2\cos^2 A - 1$$
$$= 1 - 2\sin^2 A$$

Table of standard derivatives:

$f(x)$	$f'(x)$
$\sin ax$	$a \cos ax$
$\cos ax$	$-a \sin ax$

Table of standard integrals:

$f(x)$	$\int f(x)\,dx$
$\sin ax$	$-\dfrac{1}{a}\cos ax + C$
$\cos ax$	$\dfrac{1}{a}\sin ax + C$

[Turn over

SECTION A

ALL questions should be attempted.

1. A sequence is defined by $u_{n+1} = 3u_n + 4$ with $u_1 = 2$.

   What is the value of u_3?

   A   34

   B   21

   C   18

   D   13

2. A circle has equation $x^2 + y^2 + 8x + 6y - 75 = 0$.

   What is the radius of this circle?

   A   5

   B   10

   C $\sqrt{75}$

   D $\sqrt{175}$

3. Triangle PQR has vertices at P(-3, -2), Q(-1, 4) and R(3, 6).

   PS is a median. What is the gradient of PS?

   A -2

   B $-\dfrac{7}{4}$

   C   1

   D $\dfrac{7}{4}$

4. A curve has equation $y = 5x^3 - 12x$.

   What is the gradient of the tangent at the point (1, -7)?

   A -7

   B -5

   C   3

   D   5

5. Here are two statements about the points S(2, 3) and T(5, −1):

   (1) The length of ST = 5 units;

   (2) The gradient of ST = $\dfrac{4}{3}$.

   Which of the following is true?

   A   Neither statement is correct.

   B   Only statement (1) is correct.

   C   Only statement (2) is correct.

   D   Both statements are correct.

6. A sequence is generated by the recurrence relation $u_{n+1} = 0 \cdot 7 u_n + 10$.

   What is the limit of this sequence as $n \to \infty$?

   A $\dfrac{100}{3}$

   B $\dfrac{100}{7}$

   C $\dfrac{17}{100}$

   D $\dfrac{3}{10}$

7. If the exact value of $\cos x$ is $\dfrac{1}{\sqrt{5}}$, find the exact value of $\cos 2x$.

   A $-\dfrac{3}{5}$

   B $-\dfrac{2}{\sqrt{5}}$

   C $\dfrac{2}{\sqrt{5}}$

   D $\dfrac{3}{5}$

[Turn over

8. What is the derivative of $\dfrac{1}{4x^3}$, $x \neq 0$?

A $\dfrac{1}{12x^2}$

B $-\dfrac{1}{12x^2}$

C $\dfrac{4}{x^4}$

D $-\dfrac{3}{4x^4}$

9. The line with equation $y = 2x$ intersects the circle with equation $x^2 + y^2 = 5$ at the points J and K.

What are the x-coordinates of J and K?

A $x_J = 1, x_K = -1$

B $x_J = 2, x_K = -2$

C $x_J = 1, x_K = -2$

D $x_J = -1, x_K = 2$

10. Which of the following graphs has equation $y = \log_5(x - 2)$?

A

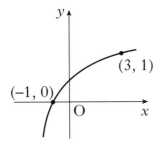

B

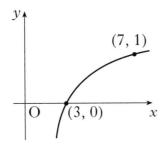

C

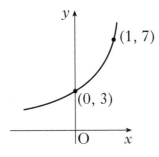

D

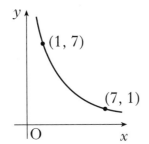

[Turn over

11. How many solutions does the equation

$$(4 \sin x - \sqrt{5})(\sin x + 1) = 0$$

have in the interval $0 \le x < 2\pi$?

A   4

B   3

C   2

D   1

12. A function f is given by $f(x) = 2x^2 - x - 9$.

Which of the following describes the nature of the roots of $f(x) = 0$?

A   No real roots

B   Equal roots

C   Real distinct roots

D   Rational distinct roots

13. k and a are given by

$$k \sin a° = 1$$
$$k \cos a° = \sqrt{3}$$

where $k > 0$ and $0 \le a < 90$.

What are the values of k and a?

	k	a
A	2	60
B	2	30
C	$\sqrt{10}$	60
D	$\sqrt{10}$	30

14. If $f(x) = 2\sin\left(3x - \frac{\pi}{2}\right) + 5$, what is the range of values of $f(x)$?

A $-1 \le f(x) \le 11$

B $2 \le f(x) \le 8$

C $3 \le f(x) \le 7$

D $-3 \le f(x) \le 7$

15. The line GH makes an angle of $\frac{\pi}{6}$ radians with the y-axis, as shown in the diagram. What is the gradient of GH?

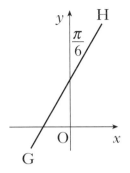

A $\sqrt{3}$

B $\frac{1}{2}$

C $\frac{1}{\sqrt{2}}$

D $\frac{\sqrt{3}}{2}$

16. The graph of $y = 4x^3 - 9x^2$ is shown in the diagram.

Which of the following gives the area of the shaded section?

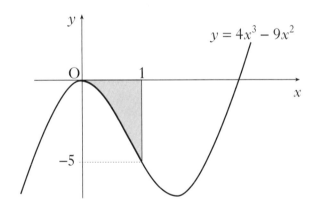

A $\left[x^4 - 3x^3 \right]_{-5}^{0}$

B $-\left[x^4 - 3x^3 \right]_{0}^{1}$

C $\left[12x^2 - 18x \right]_{-5}^{0}$

D $-\left[12x^2 - 18x \right]_{0}^{1}$

17. The vector $\boldsymbol{u}$ has components $\begin{pmatrix} -3 \\ 0 \\ 4 \end{pmatrix}$.

Which of the following is a unit vector parallel to $\boldsymbol{u}$?

A $-\dfrac{3}{5}\boldsymbol{i} + \dfrac{4}{5}\boldsymbol{k}$

B $-3\boldsymbol{i} + 4\boldsymbol{k}$

C $-\dfrac{3}{\sqrt{7}}\boldsymbol{i} + \dfrac{4}{\sqrt{7}}\boldsymbol{k}$

D $-\dfrac{1}{3}\boldsymbol{i} + \dfrac{1}{4}\boldsymbol{k}$

18. Given that $f(x) = (4 - 3x^2)^{-\frac{1}{2}}$ on a suitable domain, find $f'(x)$.

A $-3x(4 - 3x^2)^{-\frac{1}{2}}$

B $-\dfrac{1}{2}(4 - 6x)^{-\frac{3}{2}}$

C $2(4 - 3x^3)^{\frac{1}{2}}$

D $3x(4 - 3x^2)^{-\frac{3}{2}}$

19. For what values of x is $6 + x - x^2 < 0$?

A $x > 3$ only

B $x < -2$ only

C $x < -2, x > 3$

D $-3 < x < 2$

20. $A = 2\pi r^2 + 6\pi r$.

What is the rate of change of A with respect to r when $r = 2$?

A 10π

B 12π

C 14π

D 20π

[END OF SECTION A]

SECTION B

ALL questions should be attempted.

Marks

21. Triangle PQR has vertex P on the x-axis, as shown in the diagram.

    Q and R are the points (4, 6) and (8, −2) respectively.

    The equation of PQ is $6x - 7y + 18 = 0$.

    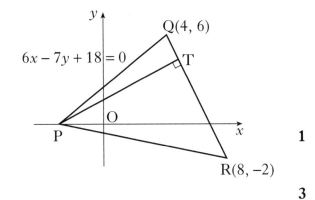

    (a) State the coordinates of P. **1**

    (b) Find the equation of the altitude of the triangle from P. **3**

    (c) The altitude from P meets the line QR at T. Find the coordinates of T. **4**

22. D, E and F have coordinates (10, −8, −15), (1, −2, −3) and (−2, 0, 1) respectively.

    (a) (i) Show that D, E and F are collinear.

      (ii) Find the ratio in which E divides DF. **4**

    (b) G has coordinates $(k, 1, 0)$.

      Given that DE is perpendicular to GE, find the value of k. **4**

23. The diagram shows a sketch of the function $y = f(x)$.

    (a) Copy the diagram and on it sketch the graph of $y = f(2x)$. **2**

    (b) On a separate diagram sketch the graph of $y = 1 - f(2x)$. **3**

    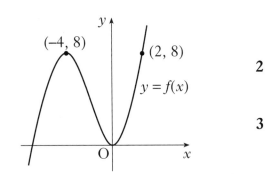

[Turn over for Question 24 on *Page twelve*

Marks

24. (a) Using the fact that $\dfrac{7\pi}{12} = \dfrac{\pi}{3} + \dfrac{\pi}{4}$, find the exact value of $\sin\left(\dfrac{7\pi}{12}\right)$.   **3**

(b) Show that $\sin(A + B) + \sin(A - B) = 2\sin A \cos B$.   **2**

(c) (i) Express $\dfrac{\pi}{12}$ in terms of $\dfrac{\pi}{3}$ and $\dfrac{\pi}{4}$.

(ii) Hence or otherwise find the exact value of $\sin\left(\dfrac{7\pi}{12}\right) + \sin\left(\dfrac{\pi}{12}\right)$.   **4**

[END OF SECTION B]

[END OF QUESTION PAPER]

X100/302

NATIONAL
QUALIFICATIONS
2009

THURSDAY, 21 MAY
10.50 AM – 12.00 NOON

MATHEMATICS
HIGHER
Paper 2

Read Carefully

1   **Calculators may be used in this paper.**

2   Full credit will be given only where the solution contains appropriate working.

3   Answers obtained by readings from scale drawings will not receive any credit.

FORMULAE LIST

Circle:

The equation $x^2 + y^2 + 2gx + 2fy + c = 0$ represents a circle centre $(-g, -f)$ and radius $\sqrt{g^2 + f^2 - c}$.

The equation $(x - a)^2 + (y - b)^2 = r^2$ represents a circle centre (a, b) and radius r.

Scalar Product: $a.b = |a|\,|b| \cos \theta$, where θ is the angle between a and b

or $a.b = a_1 b_1 + a_2 b_2 + a_3 b_3$ where $a = \begin{pmatrix} a_1 \\ a_2 \\ a_3 \end{pmatrix}$ and $b = \begin{pmatrix} b_1 \\ b_2 \\ b_3 \end{pmatrix}$.

Trigonometric formulae:

$$\sin (A \pm B) = \sin A \cos B \pm \cos A \sin B$$
$$\cos (A \pm B) = \cos A \cos B \mp \sin A \sin B$$
$$\sin 2A = 2\sin A \cos A$$
$$\cos 2A = \cos^2 A - \sin^2 A$$
$$= 2\cos^2 A - 1$$
$$= 1 - 2\sin^2 A$$

Table of standard derivatives:

$f(x)$	$f'(x)$
$\sin ax$	$a \cos ax$
$\cos ax$	$-a \sin ax$

Table of standard integrals:

$f(x)$	$\int f(x)\,dx$
$\sin ax$	$-\dfrac{1}{a} \cos ax + C$
$\cos ax$	$\dfrac{1}{a} \sin ax + C$

ALL questions should be attempted.

Marks

1. Find the coordinates of the turning points of the curve with equation $y = x^3 - 3x^2 - 9x + 12$ and determine their nature.

   8

2. Functions f and g are given by $f(x) = 3x + 1$ and $g(x) = x^2 - 2$.

   (a) (i) Find $p(x)$ where $p(x) = f(g(x))$.

   (ii) Find $q(x)$ where $q(x) = g(f(x))$.

   3

   (b) Solve $p'(x) = q'(x)$.

   3

3. (a) (i) Show that $x = 1$ is a root of $x^3 + 8x^2 + 11x - 20 = 0$.

   (ii) Hence factorise $x^3 + 8x^2 + 11x - 20$ fully.

   4

   (b) Solve $\log_2(x + 3) + \log_2(x^2 + 5x - 4) = 3$.

   5

4. (a) Show that the point P(5, 10) lies on circle C_1 with equation $(x + 1)^2 + (y - 2)^2 = 100$.

   1

   (b) PQ is a diameter of this circle as shown in the diagram. Find the equation of the tangent at Q.

   5

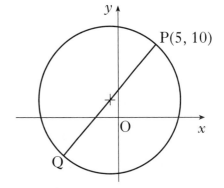

   (c) Two circles, C_2 and C_3, touch circle C_1 at Q.

   The radius of each of these circles is twice the radius of circle C_1.

   Find the equations of circles C_2 and C_3.

   4

[Turn over

Marks

5. The graphs of $y = f(x)$ and $y = g(x)$ are shown in the diagram.

   $f(x) = -4\cos(2x) + 3$ and $g(x)$ is of the form $g(x) = m\cos(nx)$.

   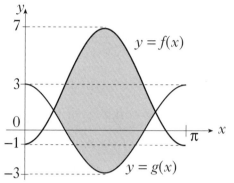

   (a) Write down the values of m and n.   **1**

   (b) Find, correct to one decimal place, the coordinates of the points of intersection of the two graphs in the interval $0 \le x \le \pi$.   **5**

   (c) Calculate the shaded area.   **6**

6. The size of the human population, N, can be modelled using the equation $N = N_0 e^{rt}$ where N_0 is the population in 2006, t is the time in years since 2006, and r is the annual rate of increase in the population.

   (a) In 2006 the population of the United Kingdom was approximately 61 million, with an annual rate of increase of 1·6%. Assuming this growth rate remains constant, what would be the population in 2020?   **2**

   (b) In 2006 the population of Scotland was approximately 5·1 million, with an annual rate of increase of 0·43%.

   Assuming this growth rate remains constant, how long would it take for Scotland's population to double in size?   **3**

7. Vectors $\boldsymbol{p}$, $\boldsymbol{q}$ and $\boldsymbol{r}$ are represented on the diagram shown where angle ADC = 30°.

   It is also given that $|\boldsymbol{p}| = 4$ and $|\boldsymbol{q}| = 3$.

   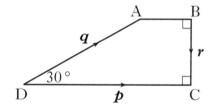

   (a) Evaluate $\boldsymbol{p}.(\boldsymbol{q} + \boldsymbol{r})$ and $\boldsymbol{r}.(\boldsymbol{p} - \boldsymbol{q})$.   **6**

   (b) Find $|\boldsymbol{q} + \boldsymbol{r}|$ and $|\boldsymbol{p} - \boldsymbol{q}|$.   **4**

[END OF QUESTION PAPER]

[BLANK PAGE]

X100/301

NATIONAL
QUALIFICATIONS
2010

FRIDAY, 21 MAY
9.00 AM – 10.30 AM

MATHEMATICS
HIGHER
Paper 1
(Non-calculator)

Read carefully

Calculators may <u>NOT</u> be used in this paper.

Section A – Questions 1–20 (40 marks)

Instructions for completion of **Section A** are given on page two.

For this section of the examination you must use an **HB pencil**.

Section B (30 marks)

1   Full credit will be given only where the solution contains appropriate working.

2   Answers obtained by readings from scale drawings will not receive any credit.

Read carefully

1 Check that the answer sheet provided is for **Mathematics Higher (Section A)**.

2 For this section of the examination you must use an **HB pencil** and, where necessary, an eraser.

3 Check that the answer sheet you have been given has **your name**, **date of birth**, **SCN** (Scottish Candidate Number) and **Centre Name** printed on it.

   Do not change any of these details.

4 If any of this information is wrong, tell the Invigilator immediately.

5 If this information is correct, **print** your name and seat number in the boxes provided.

6 The answer to each question is **either** A, B, C or D. Decide what your answer is, then, using your pencil, put a horizontal line in the space provided (see sample question below).

7 There is **only one correct** answer to each question.

8 Rough working should **not** be done on your answer sheet.

9 At the end of the exam, put the **answer sheet for Section A inside the front cover of your answer book**.

Sample Question

A curve has equation $y = x^3 - 4x$.

What is the gradient at the point where $x = 2$?

   A   8

   B   1

   C   0

   D -4

The correct answer is **A**—8. The answer **A** has been clearly marked in **pencil** with a horizontal line (see below).

Changing an answer

If you decide to change your answer, carefully erase your first answer and, using your pencil, fill in the answer you want. The answer below has been changed to **D**.

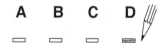

FORMULAE LIST

Circle:

The equation $x^2 + y^2 + 2gx + 2fy + c = 0$ represents a circle centre $(-g, -f)$ and radius $\sqrt{g^2 + f^2 - c}$.

The equation $(x - a)^2 + (y - b)^2 = r^2$ represents a circle centre (a, b) and radius r.

Scalar Product: $\quad$ $\mathbf{a.b} = |\mathbf{a}|\,|\mathbf{b}|\cos\theta$, where θ is the angle between $\mathbf{a}$ and $\mathbf{b}$

$\quad$ or $\quad$ $\mathbf{a.b} = a_1b_1 + a_2b_2 + a_3b_3$ where $\mathbf{a} = \begin{pmatrix} a_1 \\ a_2 \\ a_3 \end{pmatrix}$ and $\mathbf{b} = \begin{pmatrix} b_1 \\ b_2 \\ b_3 \end{pmatrix}$.

Trigonometric formulae:

$$\sin(A \pm B) = \sin A \cos B \pm \cos A \sin B$$
$$\cos(A \pm B) = \cos A \cos B \mp \sin A \sin B$$
$$\sin 2A = 2\sin A \cos A$$
$$\cos 2A = \cos^2 A - \sin^2 A$$
$$= 2\cos^2 A - 1$$
$$= 1 - 2\sin^2 A$$

Table of standard derivatives:

$f(x)$	$f'(x)$
$\sin ax$	$a\cos ax$
$\cos ax$	$-a\sin ax$

Table of standard integrals:

$f(x)$	$\int f(x)\,dx$
$\sin ax$	$-\dfrac{1}{a}\cos ax + C$
$\cos ax$	$\dfrac{1}{a}\sin ax + C$

[Turn over

SECTION A

ALL questions should be attempted.

1. A line L is perpendicular to the line with equation $2x - 3y - 6 = 0$.

   What is the gradient of the line L?

   A $-\dfrac{3}{2}$

   B $-\dfrac{1}{2}$

   C $\dfrac{2}{3}$

   D 2

2. A sequence is defined by the recurrence relation $u_{n+1} = 2u_n + 3$ and $u_0 = 1$.

   What is the value of u_2?

   A   7

   B   10

   C   13

   D   16

3. Given that $\mathbf{u} = \begin{pmatrix} 2 \\ 0 \\ 1 \end{pmatrix}$ and $\mathbf{v} = \begin{pmatrix} -1 \\ 2 \\ 4 \end{pmatrix}$, find $3\mathbf{u} - 2\mathbf{v}$ in component form.

   A $\begin{pmatrix} 4 \\ -1 \\ -5 \end{pmatrix}$

   B $\begin{pmatrix} 4 \\ -4 \\ 11 \end{pmatrix}$

   C $\begin{pmatrix} 8 \\ -1 \\ 5 \end{pmatrix}$

   D $\begin{pmatrix} 8 \\ -4 \\ -5 \end{pmatrix}$

4. The diagram shows the graph with equation of the form $y = a\cos bx$ for $0 \le x \le 2\pi$.

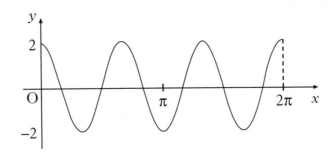

What is the equation of this graph?

A $y = 2\cos 3x$

B $y = 2\cos 2x$

C $y = 3\cos 2x$

D $y = 4\cos 3x$

5. When $x^2 + 8x + 3$ is written in the form $(x + p)^2 + q$, what is the value of q?

A -19

B -13

C -5

D 19

[Turn over

6. The roots of the equation $kx^2 - 3x + 2 = 0$ are equal.

What is the value of k?

A $\quad -\dfrac{9}{8}$

B $\quad -\dfrac{8}{9}$

C $\quad \dfrac{8}{9}$

D $\quad \dfrac{9}{8}$

7. A sequence is generated by the recurrence relation $u_{n+1} = \dfrac{1}{4}u_n + 7$, with $u_0 = -2$.

What is the limit of this sequence as $n \to \infty$?

A $\quad \dfrac{1}{28}$

B $\quad \dfrac{28}{5}$

C $\quad \dfrac{28}{3}$

D $\quad 28$

8. The equation of the circle shown in the diagram is $x^2 + y^2 - 6x - 10y + 9 = 0$.

The x-axis and the line l are parallel tangents to the circle.

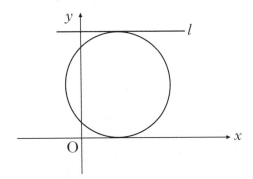

What is the equation of line l?

A $y = 5$

B $y = 10$

C $y = 18$

D $y = 20$

9. Find $\int (2x^{-4} + \cos 5x)\, dx$.

A $-\dfrac{2}{5}x^{-5} - 5\sin 5x + c$

B $-\dfrac{2}{5}x^{-5} + \dfrac{1}{5}\sin 5x + c$

C $-\dfrac{2}{3}x^{-3} + \dfrac{1}{5}\sin 5x + c$

D $-\dfrac{2}{3}x^{-3} - 5\sin 5x + c$

10. The vectors $x\mathbf{i} + 5\mathbf{j} + 7\mathbf{k}$ and $-3\mathbf{i} + 2\mathbf{j} - \mathbf{k}$ are perpendicular.

What is the value of x?

A   0

B   1

C $\dfrac{4}{3}$

D $\dfrac{10}{3}$

[Turn over

11. Functions f and g are defined on suitable domains by $f(x) = \cos x$ and $g(x) = x + \dfrac{\pi}{6}$.

What is the value of $f\left(g\left(\dfrac{\pi}{6}\right)\right)$?

A $\dfrac{1}{2} + \dfrac{\pi}{6}$

B $\dfrac{\sqrt{3}}{2} + \dfrac{\pi}{6}$

C $\dfrac{\sqrt{3}}{2}$

D $\dfrac{1}{2}$

12. If $f(x) = \dfrac{1}{\sqrt[5]{x}}$, $x \neq 0$, what is $f'(x)$?

A $-\dfrac{1}{5}x^{-\frac{6}{5}}$

B $-\dfrac{1}{5}x^{-\frac{4}{5}}$

C $-\dfrac{5}{2}x^{-\frac{7}{2}}$

D $-\dfrac{5}{2}x^{-\frac{3}{2}}$

13. Which of the following diagrams shows a parabola with equation $y = ax^2 + bx + c$, where

- $a > 0$
- $b^2 - 4ac > 0$?

A

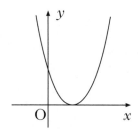

B

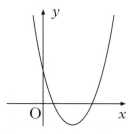

C

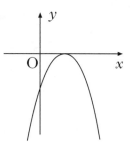

D

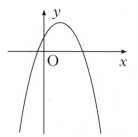

[Turn over

14. The diagram shows graphs with equations $y = 14 - x^2$ and $y = 2x^2 + 2$.

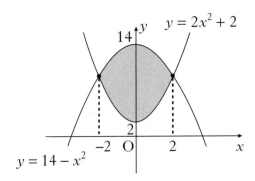

Which of the following represents the shaded area?

A $\displaystyle\int_{2}^{14} (12 - 3x^2)\,dx$

B $\displaystyle\int_{2}^{14} (3x^2 - 12)\,dx$

C $\displaystyle\int_{-2}^{2} (12 - 3x^2)\,dx$

D $\displaystyle\int_{-2}^{2} (3x^2 - 12)\,dx$

15. The derivative of a function f is given by $f'(x) = x^2 - 9$.

Here are two statements about f:

(1) f is increasing at $x = 1$;

(2) f is stationary at $x = -3$.

Which of the following is true?

A Neither statement is correct.

B Only statement (1) is correct.

C Only statement (2) is correct.

D Both statements are correct.

16. The diagram shows the graph with equation $y = k(x-1)^2(x+t)$.

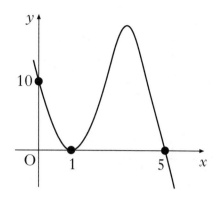

What are the values of k and t?

	k	t
A	-2	-5
B	-2	5
C	2	-5
D	2	5

17. If $s(t) = t^2 - 5t + 8$, what is the rate of change of s with respect to t when $t = 3$?

A -5

B 1

C 2

D 9

18. What is the solution of $x^2 + 4x > 0$, where x is a real number?

A $-4 < x < 0$

B $x < -4, x > 0$

C $0 < x < 4$

D $x < 0, x > 4$

[Turn over

19. The diagram shows the graph of $y = f(x)$ where f is a logarithmic function.

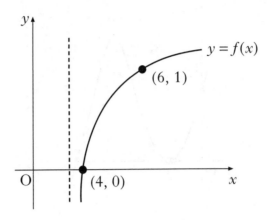

What is $f(x)$?

A $f(x) = \log_6(x - 3)$

B $f(x) = \log_3(x + 3)$

C $f(x) = \log_3(x - 3)$

D $f(x) = \log_6(x + 3)$

20. The diagram shows the graph of $y = f(2x) - 3$.

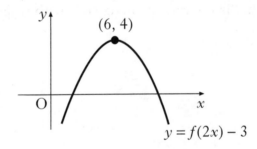

What are the coordinates of the turning point on the graph of $y = f(x)$?

A $(12, 7)$

B $(12, 1)$

C $(3, 7)$

D $(3, 1)$

[END OF SECTION A]

Marks

SECTION B

ALL questions should be attempted.

21. Triangle ABC has vertices A(4, 0), B(−4, 16) and C(18, 20), as shown in the diagram opposite.

    Medians AP and CR intersect at the point T(6, 12).

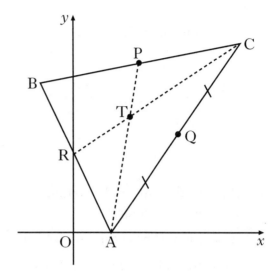

    (a) Find the equation of median BQ.   3

    (b) Verify that T lies on BQ.   1

    (c) Find the ratio in which T divides BQ.   2

22. (a) (i) Show that $(x - 1)$ is a factor of $f(x) = 2x^3 + x^2 - 8x + 5$.

    (ii) Hence factorise $f(x)$ fully.   5

    (b) Solve $2x^3 + x^2 - 8x + 5 = 0$.   1

    (c) The line with equation $y = 2x - 3$ is a tangent to the curve with equation $y = 2x^3 + x^2 - 6x + 2$ at the point G.

    Find the coordinates of G.   5

    (d) This tangent meets the curve again at the point H.

    Write down the coordinates of H.   1

[Turn over for Question 23 on *Page fourteen*

Marks

23. (*a*) Diagram 1 shows a right angled triangle, where the line OA has equation $3x - 2y = 0$.

  (i) Show that $\tan a = \dfrac{3}{2}$.

  (ii) Find the value of $\sin a$.

4

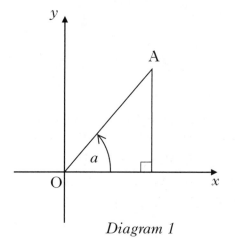

Diagram 1

(*b*) A second right angled triangle is added as shown in Diagram 2.

The line OB has equation $3x - 4y = 0$.

Find the values of $\sin b$ and $\cos b$.

4

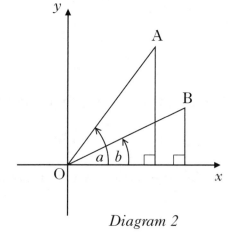

Diagram 2

(*c*) (i) Find the value of $\sin(a - b)$.

  (ii) State the value of $\sin(b - a)$.

4

[*END OF SECTION B*]

[*END OF QUESTION PAPER*]

X100/302

NATIONAL
QUALIFICATIONS
2010

FRIDAY, 21 MAY
10.50 AM – 12.00 NOON

MATHEMATICS
HIGHER
Paper 2

Read Carefully

1   **Calculators may be used in this paper.**

2   Full credit will be given only where the solution contains appropriate working.

3   Answers obtained by readings from scale drawings will not receive any credit.

FORMULAE LIST

Circle:

The equation $x^2 + y^2 + 2gx + 2fy + c = 0$ represents a circle centre $(-g, -f)$ and radius $\sqrt{g^2 + f^2 - c}$.

The equation $(x - a)^2 + (y - b)^2 = r^2$ represents a circle centre (a, b) and radius r.

Scalar Product: $\mathbf{a.b} = |\mathbf{a}|\,|\mathbf{b}|\cos\theta$, where θ is the angle between $\mathbf{a}$ and $\mathbf{b}$

or $\mathbf{a.b} = a_1b_1 + a_2b_2 + a_3b_3$ where $\mathbf{a} = \begin{pmatrix} a_1 \\ a_2 \\ a_3 \end{pmatrix}$ and $\mathbf{b} = \begin{pmatrix} b_1 \\ b_2 \\ b_3 \end{pmatrix}$.

Trigonometric formulae:
$$\sin(A \pm B) = \sin A \cos B \pm \cos A \sin B$$
$$\cos(A \pm B) = \cos A \cos B \mp \sin A \sin B$$
$$\sin 2A = 2\sin A \cos A$$
$$\cos 2A = \cos^2 A - \sin^2 A$$
$$= 2\cos^2 A - 1$$
$$= 1 - 2\sin^2 A$$

Table of standard derivatives:

$f(x)$	$f'(x)$
$\sin ax$	$a\cos ax$
$\cos ax$	$-a\sin ax$

Table of standard integrals:

$f(x)$	$\int f(x)\,dx$
$\sin ax$	$-\dfrac{1}{a}\cos ax + C$
$\cos ax$	$\dfrac{1}{a}\sin ax + C$

Marks

ALL questions should be attempted.

1. The diagram shows a cuboid OPQR,STUV relative to the coordinate axes.

P is the point (4, 0, 0),
Q is (4, 2, 0) and U is (4, 2, 3).

M is the midpoint of OR.

N is the point on UQ such that
$UN = \frac{1}{3}UQ$.

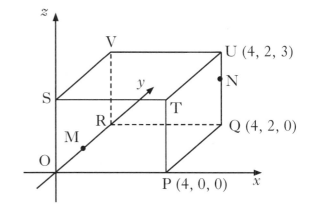

(a) State the coordinates of M and N. 2

(b) Express $\overrightarrow{VM}$ and $\overrightarrow{VN}$ in component form. 2

(c) Calculate the size of angle MVN. 5

2. (a) $12\cos x° - 5\sin x°$ can be expressed in the form $k\cos(x + a)°$, where $k > 0$ and $0 \le a < 360$.

Calculate the values of k and a. 4

(b) (i) Hence state the maximum and minimum values of $12\cos x° - 5\sin x°$.

(ii) Determine the values of x, in the interval $0 \le x < 360$, at which these maximum and minimum values occur. 3

[Turn over

Marks

3. (*a*) (i) Show that the line with equation $y = 3 - x$ is a tangent to the circle with equation $x^2 + y^2 + 14x + 4y - 19 = 0$.

   (ii) Find the coordinates of the point of contact, P.   **5**

(*b*) Relative to a suitable set of coordinate axes, the diagram below shows the circle from (*a*) and a second smaller circle with centre C.

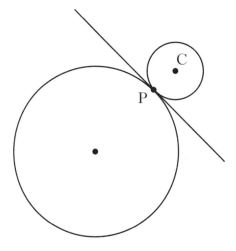

The line $y = 3 - x$ is a common tangent at the point P.

The radius of the larger circle is three times the radius of the smaller circle.

Find the equation of the smaller circle.   **6**

4. Solve $2 \cos 2x - 5 \cos x - 4 = 0$ for $0 \le x < 2\pi$.   **5**

Marks

5. The parabolas with equations $y = 10 - x^2$ and $y = \frac{2}{5}(10 - x^2)$ are shown in the diagram below.

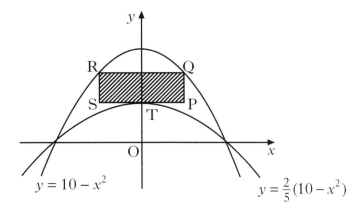

A rectangle PQRS is placed between the two parabolas as shown, so that:

- Q and R lie on the upper parabola;
- RQ and SP are parallel to the x-axis;
- T, the turning point of the lower parabola, lies on SP.

(a) (i) If TP = x units, find an expression for the length of PQ.

(ii) Hence show that the area, A, of rectangle PQRS is given by

$$A(x) = 12x - 2x^3.$$

3

(b) Find the maximum area of this rectangle.

6

[Turn over for Questions 6 and 7 on *Page six*

Marks

6. (*a*) A curve has equation $y = (2x - 9)^{\frac{1}{2}}$.

   Show that the equation of the tangent to this curve at the point where $x = 9$ is $y = \frac{1}{3}x$.   **5**

   (*b*) Diagram 1 shows part of the curve and the tangent.

   The curve cuts the *x*-axis at the point A.

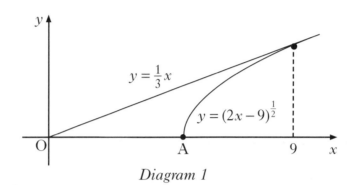

Diagram 1

   Find the coordinates of point A.   **1**

   (*c*) Calculate the shaded area shown in diagram 2.   **7**

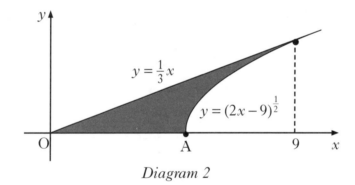

Diagram 2

7. (*a*) Given that $\log_4 x = \text{P}$, show that $\log_{16} x = \frac{1}{2}\text{P}$.   **3**

   (*b*) Solve $\log_3 x + \log_9 x = 12$.   **3**

[*END OF QUESTION PAPER*]

[BLANK PAGE]

X100/301

| NATIONAL QUALIFICATIONS 2011 | WEDNESDAY, 18 MAY 9.00 AM – 10.30 AM | MATHEMATICS HIGHER Paper 1 (Non-calculator) |

Read carefully

Calculators may <u>NOT</u> be used in this paper.

Section A – Questions 1–20 (40 marks)

Instructions for completion of **Section A** are given on page two.

For this section of the examination you must use an **HB pencil**.

Section B (30 marks)

1   Full credit will be given only where the solution contains appropriate working.

2   Answers obtained by readings from scale drawings will not receive any credit.

Read carefully

1 Check that the answer sheet provided is for **Mathematics Higher (Section A)**.

2 For this section of the examination you must use an **HB pencil** and, where necessary, an eraser.

3 Check that the answer sheet you have been given has **your name, date of birth, SCN** (Scottish Candidate Number) and **Centre Name** printed on it.

   Do not change any of these details.

4 If any of this information is wrong, tell the Invigilator immediately.

5 If this information is correct, **print** your name and seat number in the boxes provided.

6 The answer to each question is **either** A, B, C or D. Decide what your answer is, then, using your pencil, put a horizontal line in the space provided (see sample question below).

7 There is **only one correct** answer to each question.

8 Rough working should **not** be done on your answer sheet.

9 At the end of the exam, put the **answer sheet for Section A inside the front cover of your answer book**.

Sample Question

A curve has equation $y = x^3 - 4x$.

What is the gradient at the point where $x = 2$?

   A   8

   B   1

   C   0

   D −4

The correct answer is **A**—8. The answer **A** has been clearly marked in **pencil** with a horizontal line (see below).

Changing an answer

If you decide to change your answer, carefully erase your first answer and, using your pencil, fill in the answer you want. The answer below has been changed to **D**.

FORMULAE LIST

Circle:

The equation $x^2 + y^2 + 2gx + 2fy + c = 0$ represents a circle centre $(-g, -f)$ and radius $\sqrt{g^2 + f^2 - c}$.

The equation $(x - a)^2 + (y - b)^2 = r^2$ represents a circle centre (a, b) and radius r.

Scalar Product: $\mathbf{a}.\mathbf{b} = |\mathbf{a}|\,|\mathbf{b}|\cos\theta$, where θ is the angle between $\mathbf{a}$ and $\mathbf{b}$

or $\mathbf{a}.\mathbf{b} = a_1b_1 + a_2b_2 + a_3b_3$ where $\mathbf{a} = \begin{pmatrix} a_1 \\ a_2 \\ a_3 \end{pmatrix}$ and $\mathbf{b} = \begin{pmatrix} b_1 \\ b_2 \\ b_3 \end{pmatrix}$.

Trigonometric formulae:

$$\sin(A \pm B) = \sin A \cos B \pm \cos A \sin B$$
$$\cos(A \pm B) = \cos A \cos B \mp \sin A \sin B$$
$$\sin 2A = 2\sin A \cos A$$
$$\cos 2A = \cos^2 A - \sin^2 A$$
$$= 2\cos^2 A - 1$$
$$= 1 - 2\sin^2 A$$

Table of standard derivatives:

$f(x)$	$f'(x)$
$\sin ax$	$a\cos ax$
$\cos ax$	$-a\sin ax$

Table of standard integrals:

$f(x)$	$\int f(x)\,dx$
$\sin ax$	$-\dfrac{1}{a}\cos ax + C$
$\cos ax$	$\dfrac{1}{a}\sin ax + C$

[Turn over

SECTION A

ALL questions should be attempted.

1. Given that $\mathbf{p} = \begin{pmatrix} 2 \\ 5 \\ -7 \end{pmatrix}$, $\mathbf{q} = \begin{pmatrix} 1 \\ 0 \\ -1 \end{pmatrix}$ and $\mathbf{r} = \begin{pmatrix} -4 \\ 2 \\ 0 \end{pmatrix}$, express $2\mathbf{p} - \mathbf{q} - \frac{1}{2}\mathbf{r}$ in component form.

   A $\begin{pmatrix} 1 \\ 9 \\ -15 \end{pmatrix}$

   B $\begin{pmatrix} 1 \\ 11 \\ -13 \end{pmatrix}$

   C $\begin{pmatrix} 5 \\ 9 \\ -13 \end{pmatrix}$

   D $\begin{pmatrix} 5 \\ 11 \\ -15 \end{pmatrix}$

2. A line l has equation $3y + 2x = 6$.

   What is the gradient of any line parallel to l?

   A -2

   B $-\dfrac{2}{3}$

   C $\dfrac{3}{2}$

   D 2

3. The diagram shows the graph of $y = f(x)$.

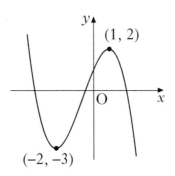

Which of the following shows the graph of $y = f(x + 2) - 1$?

A

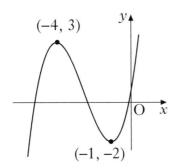

B

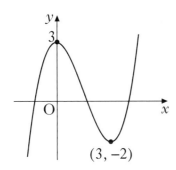

C

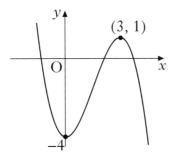

D

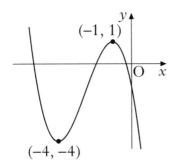

[Turn over

4. A tangent to the curve with equation $y = x^3 - 2x$ is drawn at the point $(2, 4)$.

What is the gradient of this tangent?

A   2

B   3

C   4

D   10

5. If $x^2 - 8x + 7$ is written in the form $(x - p)^2 + q$, what is the value of q?

A   −9

B   −1

C   7

D   23

6. The point P(2, −3) lies on the circle with centre C as shown.

The gradient of CP is −2.

What is the equation of the tangent at P?

A $y + 3 = -2(x - 2)$

B $y - 3 = -2(x + 2)$

C $y + 3 = \frac{1}{2}(x - 2)$

D $y - 3 = \frac{1}{2}(x + 2)$

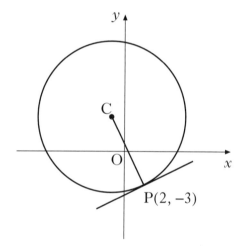

7. A function f is defined on the set of real numbers by $f(x) = x^3 - x^2 + x + 3$.

What is the remainder when $f(x)$ is divided by $(x - 1)$?

A   0

B   2

C   3

D   4

8. A line makes an angle of 30° with the positive direction of the x-axis as shown.

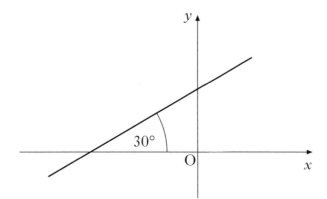

What is the gradient of the line?

A $\dfrac{1}{\sqrt{3}}$

B $\dfrac{1}{\sqrt{2}}$

C $\dfrac{1}{2}$

D $\dfrac{\sqrt{3}}{2}$

9. The discriminant of a quadratic equation is 23.

Here are two statements about this quadratic equation:

(1) the roots are real;

(2) the roots are rational.

Which of the following is true?

A   Neither statement is correct.

B   Only statement (1) is correct.

C   Only statement (2) is correct.

D   Both statements are correct.

[Turn over

10. Solve $2\cos x = \sqrt{3}$ for x, where $0 \le x < 2\pi$.

A $\dfrac{\pi}{3}$ and $\dfrac{5\pi}{3}$

B $\dfrac{\pi}{3}$ and $\dfrac{2\pi}{3}$

C $\dfrac{\pi}{6}$ and $\dfrac{5\pi}{6}$

D $\dfrac{\pi}{6}$ and $\dfrac{11\pi}{6}$

11. Find $\displaystyle\int\left(4x^{\frac{1}{2}} + x^{-3}\right)dx$, where $x > 0$.

A $2x^{-\frac{1}{2}} - 3x^{-4} + c$

B $2x^{-\frac{1}{2}} - \dfrac{1}{2}x^{-2} + c$

C $\dfrac{8}{3}x^{\frac{3}{2}} - 3x^{-4} + c$

D $\dfrac{8}{3}x^{\frac{3}{2}} - \dfrac{1}{2}x^{-2} + c$

12. The diagram shows two right-angled triangles with sides and angles as given.

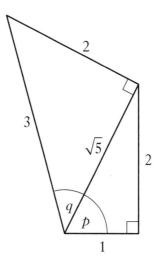

What is the value of $\sin(p + q)$?

A $\dfrac{2}{\sqrt{5}} + \dfrac{2}{3}$

B $\dfrac{2}{\sqrt{5}} + \dfrac{\sqrt{5}}{3}$

C $\dfrac{2}{3} + \dfrac{2}{3\sqrt{5}}$

D $\dfrac{4}{3\sqrt{5}} + \dfrac{1}{3}$

13. Given that $f(x) = 4 \sin 3x$, find $f'(0)$.

A   0

B   1

C   12

D   36

[Turn over

14. An equilateral triangle of side 3 units is shown.

The vectors **p** and **q** are as represented in the diagram.

What is the value of **p.q**?

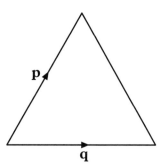

A   9

B $\dfrac{9}{2}$

C $\dfrac{9}{\sqrt{2}}$

D   0

15. Given that the points S(–4, 5, 1), T(–16, –4, 16) and U(–24, –10, 26) are collinear, calculate the ratio in which T divides SU.

A   2 : 3

B   3 : 2

C   2 : 5

D   3 : 5

16. Find $\displaystyle\int \dfrac{1}{3x^4}\,dx$, where $x \neq 0$.

A $-\dfrac{1}{9x^3} + c$

B $-\dfrac{1}{x^3} + c$

C $\dfrac{1}{x^3} + c$

D $\dfrac{1}{12x^3} + c$

17. The diagram shows the graph of a cubic.

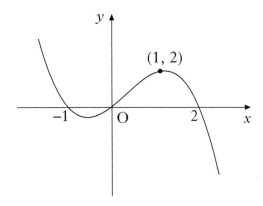

What is the equation of this cubic?

A $\quad y = -x(x + 1)(x - 2)$

B $\quad y = -x(x - 1)(x + 2)$

C $\quad y = x(x + 1)(x - 2)$

D $\quad y = x(x - 1)(x + 2)$

18. If $f(x) = (x - 3)(x + 5)$, for what values of x is the graph of $y = f(x)$ above the x-axis?

A $\quad -5 < x < 3$

B $\quad -3 < x < 5$

C $\quad x < -5, x > 3$

D $\quad x < -3, x > 5$

[Turn over

19. Which of the following diagrams represents the graph with equation $\log_3 y = x$?

A

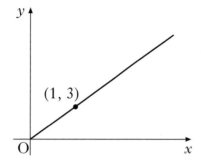

B

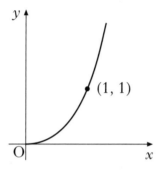

C

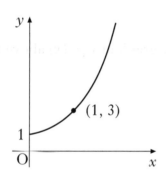

D

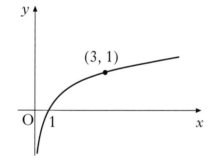

20. On a suitable domain, D, a function g is defined by $g(x) = \sin^2 \sqrt{x-2}$.

Which of the following gives the real values of x in D and the corresponding values of $g(x)$?

A $\quad x \geq 0 \quad$ and $\quad -1 \leq g(x) \leq 1$

B $\quad x \geq 0 \quad$ and $\quad 0 \leq g(x) \leq 1$

C $\quad x \geq 2 \quad$ and $\quad -1 \leq g(x) \leq 1$

D $\quad x \geq 2 \quad$ and $\quad 0 \leq g(x) \leq 1$

[END OF SECTION A]

[Turn over for SECTION B

Marks

SECTION B

ALL questions should be attempted.

21. A quadrilateral has vertices A(–1, 8), B(7, 12), C(8, 5) and D(2, –3) as shown in the diagram.

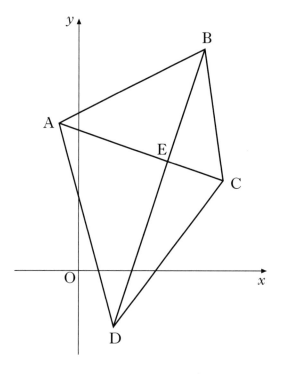

(a) Find the equation of diagonal BD. 2

(b) The equation of diagonal AC is $x + 3y = 23$.

Find the coordinates of E, the point of intersection of the diagonals. 3

(c) (i) Find the equation of the perpendicular bisector of AB.

(ii) Show that this line passes through E. 5

Marks

22. A function f is defined on the set of real numbers by $f(x) = (x - 2)(x^2 + 1)$.

    (*a*) Find where the graph of $y = f(x)$ cuts:

       (i) the x-axis;

       (ii) the y-axis.   **2**

    (*b*) Find the coordinates of the stationary points on the curve with equation $y = f(x)$ and determine their nature.   **8**

    (*c*) On separate diagrams sketch the graphs of:

       (i) $y = f(x)$;

       (ii) $y = -f(x)$.   **3**

23. (*a*) Solve $\cos 2x° - 3\cos x° + 2 = 0$ for $0 \le x < 360$.   **5**

    (*b*) Hence solve $\cos 4x° - 3\cos 2x° + 2 = 0$ for $0 \le x < 360$.   **2**

[END OF SECTION B]

[END OF QUESTION PAPER]

[BLANK PAGE]

X100/302

NATIONAL
QUALIFICATIONS
2011

WEDNESDAY, 18 MAY
10.50 AM – 12.00 NOON

MATHEMATICS
HIGHER
Paper 2

Read Carefully

1   **Calculators may be used in this paper.**

2   Full credit will be given only where the solution contains appropriate working.

3   Answers obtained by readings from scale drawings will not receive any credit.

FORMULAE LIST

Circle:

The equation $x^2 + y^2 + 2gx + 2fy + c = 0$ represents a circle centre $(-g, -f)$ and radius $\sqrt{g^2 + f^2 - c}$.

The equation $(x - a)^2 + (y - b)^2 = r^2$ represents a circle centre (a, b) and radius r.

Scalar Product: $\mathbf{a.b} = |\mathbf{a}|\,|\mathbf{b}|\cos\theta$, where θ is the angle between $\mathbf{a}$ and $\mathbf{b}$

or $\mathbf{a.b} = a_1b_1 + a_2b_2 + a_3b_3$ where $\mathbf{a} = \begin{pmatrix} a_1 \\ a_2 \\ a_3 \end{pmatrix}$ and $\mathbf{b} = \begin{pmatrix} b_1 \\ b_2 \\ b_3 \end{pmatrix}$.

Trigonometric formulae:
$$\sin(A \pm B) = \sin A \cos B \pm \cos A \sin B$$
$$\cos(A \pm B) = \cos A \cos B \mp \sin A \sin B$$
$$\sin 2A = 2\sin A \cos A$$
$$\cos 2A = \cos^2 A - \sin^2 A$$
$$= 2\cos^2 A - 1$$
$$= 1 - 2\sin^2 A$$

Table of standard derivatives:

$f(x)$	$f'(x)$
$\sin ax$	$a\cos ax$
$\cos ax$	$-a\sin ax$

Table of standard integrals:

$f(x)$	$\int f(x)\,dx$
$\sin ax$	$-\dfrac{1}{a}\cos ax + C$
$\cos ax$	$\dfrac{1}{a}\sin ax + C$

Marks

ALL questions should be attempted.

1. D,OABC is a square based pyramid as shown in the diagram below.

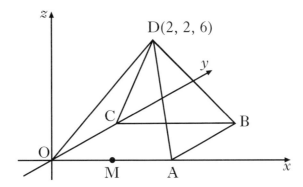

O is the origin, D is the point (2, 2, 6) and OA = 4 units.

M is the mid-point of OA.

(a) State the coordinates of B. — 1

(b) Express $\overrightarrow{DB}$ and $\overrightarrow{DM}$ in component form. — 3

(c) Find the size of angle BDM. — 5

2. Functions f, g and h are defined on the set of real numbers by

- $f(x) = x^3 - 1$
- $g(x) = 3x + 1$
- $h(x) = 4x - 5$.

(a) Find $g(f(x))$. — 2

(b) Show that $g(f(x)) + xh(x) = 3x^3 + 4x^2 - 5x - 2$. — 1

(c) (i) Show that $(x - 1)$ is a factor of $3x^3 + 4x^2 - 5x - 2$.

(ii) Factorise $3x^3 + 4x^2 - 5x - 2$ fully. — 5

(d) Hence solve $g(f(x)) + xh(x) = 0$. — 1

[Turn over

Marks

3. (*a*) A sequence is defined by $u_{n+1} = -\frac{1}{2}u_n$ with $u_0 = -16$.

Write down the values of u_1 and u_2. **1**

(*b*) A second sequence is given by $4, 5, 7, 11, \ldots$.

It is generated by the recurrence relation $v_{n+1} = pv_n + q$ with $v_1 = 4$.

Find the values of p and q. **3**

(*c*) Either the sequence in (*a*) or the sequence in (*b*) has a limit.

(i) Calculate this limit.

(ii) Why does the other sequence not have a limit? **3**

4. The diagram shows the curve with equation $y = x^3 - x^2 - 4x + 4$ and the line with equation $y = 2x + 4$.

The curve and the line intersect at the points $(-2, 0)$, $(0, 4)$ and $(3, 10)$.

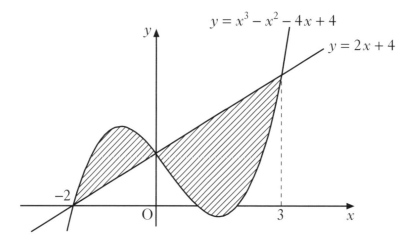

Calculate the total shaded area. **10**

Marks

5. Variables x and y are related by the equation $y = kx^n$.

   The graph of $\log_2 y$ against $\log_2 x$ is a straight line through the points $(0, 5)$ and $(4, 7)$, as shown in the diagram.

   Find the values of k and n.

   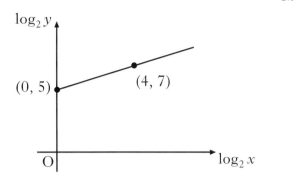

   5

6. (a) The expression $3\sin x - 5\cos x$ can be written in the form $R\sin(x+a)$ where $R > 0$ and $0 \le a < 2\pi$.

   Calculate the values of R and a. **4**

   (b) Hence find the value of t, where $0 \le t \le 2$, for which

   $$\int_0^t (3\cos x + 5\sin x)\,dx = 3.$$

   7

7. Circle C_1 has equation $(x + 1)^2 + (y - 1)^2 = 121$.

   A circle C_2 with equation $x^2 + y^2 - 4x + 6y + p = 0$ is drawn inside C_1.

   The circles have no points of contact.

   What is the range of values of p? **9**

[END OF QUESTION PAPER]

[BLANK PAGE]

SQA HIGHER
MATHEMATICS 2007–2011

MATHEMATICS HIGHER UNITS 1, 2 AND 3 PAPER 1 (NON-CALCULATOR) 2007

1. $3x - y + 7 = 0$

2. $C(7, 7, 8)$

3. $(a)\ g(f(x)) = g(x^2 + 1) = -2x^2 - 1$

   $(b)\ g(g(x)) = g(1 - 2x) = 4x - 1$

4. $k < -\dfrac{1}{4}$

5. $(x - 15)^2 + (y - 8)^2 = 4$

6. $x = 90, 270$

7. $(a)\ u_1 = 16$
   $u_2 = 20$
   $u_3 = 21$

   $(b)\ $ (i) $-1 < \dfrac{1}{4} < 1$

   (ii) $k = \dfrac{64}{3}$

8. $(a)\ f(3) = 0$ so cuts x-axis at $(3,0)$

   $(b)\ A(2, 0)$

   $(c)\ \dfrac{22}{3}$

9. $(a)\ (-\sqrt{3}, 0), (0, 0), (\sqrt{3}, 0)$

   (b) maximum turning point $(1, 2)$
   minimum turning point $(-1, -2)$

   (c)

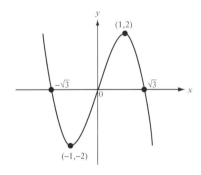

10. $3x\,(3x^2 + 2)^{-\frac{1}{2}}$

11. $(a)\ f(x) = 2\cos\left(x - \dfrac{\pi}{6}\right)$

(b)

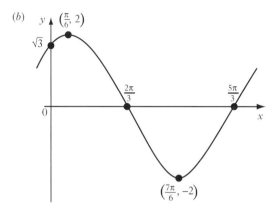

MATHEMATICS HIGHER
UNITS 1, 2 AND 3 PAPER 2
2007

1. (a) G = (0, 2, 2)

    (b) $\mathbf{p} = \begin{pmatrix} 0 \\ 1 \\ 1 \end{pmatrix}$

    $\mathbf{q} = \begin{pmatrix} 1 \\ 2 \\ 1 \end{pmatrix}$

    (c) $30°$ or $\frac{\pi}{6}$ radians

2. (a) $\frac{1}{\sqrt{2}}$

    (b) (i) $\frac{4}{5}$

    (ii) $\cos 2d = \cos^2 d - \sin^2 d$

    $= \left(\frac{3}{\sqrt{10}}\right)^2 - \left(\frac{1}{\sqrt{10}}\right)^2$

    $= \frac{9}{10} - \frac{1}{10}$

    $= \frac{8}{10}$

    $= \frac{4}{5}$

3. $x^2 + (6 - 2x)^2 + 6x - 4(6 - 2x) - 7 = 0$
    $x^2 + 36 - 24x + 4x^2 + 6x - 24 + 8x - 7 = 0$
    $5x^2 - 10x + 5 = 0$
    $5(x^2 - 1) = 0$
    Equal roots so line is tangent.
    Point of contact (1, 4)

4. (a) $a = 2, b = 3, c = -1$

    (b) $x_p = 50°$

5. (a) Q = (12, 10)

    (b) P = (4, 10)

    (c) C = (8, 11)

6. (a) (i) $ST = \sqrt{200}$

    (ii) $Length = \sqrt{200} - 2x$
    $(\sqrt{200} - 2x) \times x$ and complete proof

    (b) $x = 10\sqrt{\frac{2}{4}}$

    $length = 5\sqrt{2}$

7. 0·36

8. $a = 12·2$

9. (a)

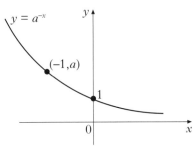

(b)

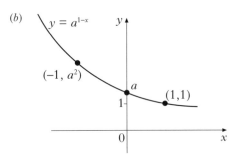

10. (a) (i) $a = 2$ and $b = 4$

    (ii) $k = \frac{3}{4}$

    (b) $y = \frac{1}{4} x^3 - \frac{9}{4} x^2 + 6x + 6$

11. (a) $a = \frac{1}{2}$

    (b) $b = \frac{3}{2}$

    (c) $\log_{10} y = \log_{10} (3 \times 4^x)$

    $\log_{10} y = \log_{10} 3 + \log_{10} 4^x$

    $\log_{10} y = x \log_{10} 4 + \log_{10} 3$

    so $gradient = \log_{10} 4$ ($\approx$

MATHEMATICS HIGHER
UNITS 1, 2 AND 3 PAPER 1 (NON-CALCULATOR)
2008 SQP

SECTION A

1. B	**2.** A	**3.** C	**4.** C
5. A	**6.** A	**7.** C	**8.** A
9. B	**10.** C	**11.** C	**12.** B
13. A	**14.** D	**15.** A	**16.** C
17. A	**18.** B	**19.** D	**20.** C

SECTION B

21. (a) A: $u_{n+1} = 0.3u_n + 300$
   B: $v_{n+1} = 0.2v_n + 350$

   (b) A: $L_A = 428$
   B: $L_B = 437$
   since $428 < 437$
   product A more effective in long term

22. (a) Maximum t. pt at $(2, 0)$
   Minimum t. pt at $(4, -4)$

   (b) (i)   Multiply out brackets
   (b) (ii)

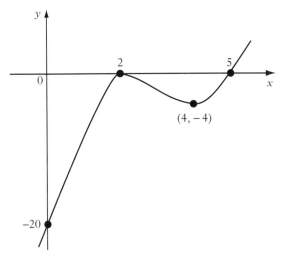

23. $x_A = -10$, $x_B = 1$ and $x_C = 3$

24. $p = \dfrac{5\pi}{6}$

MATHEMATICS HIGHER
UNITS 1, 2 AND 3 PAPER 2
2008 SQP

1. (a) $3x + y - 19 = 0$
   (b) $x - y - 1 = 0$
   (c) P(5, 4)
   (d) $m_{PQ} = -1$ and $m_{CB} = -1$ so PQ and CB are parallel

2. (a) AB = 1, AD = 4 and AE = 5

   (b) $\overrightarrow{HB}\begin{pmatrix} 1 \\ -4 \\ -5 \end{pmatrix}$ and $\overrightarrow{HC}\begin{pmatrix} 1 \\ 0 \\ -5 \end{pmatrix}$

   so $\angle HBC = 38.1°$ or 0.665 radians

3. (a) $13 \sin (x - 67.4)°$
   (b) 97.4, 217.4

4. (a) $2x - y + 1 = 0$
   (b) Q$(-2, -3)$
   (c) 2 : 1

5. (a) $\dfrac{500}{3}$

   (b) $A_{max} = 125 = \dfrac{3}{4}$ of enclosed area

6. (a) $k = 0.0004332$
   (b) 25%

7. BD $= 3\sqrt{5}$ units

MATHEMATICS HIGHER UNITS 1, 2 AND 3 PAPER 1 (NON-CALCULATOR) 2008

SECTION A

1. C	**2.** D	**3.** C	**4.** B
5. A	**6.** B	**7.** C	**8.** D
9. B	**10.** A	**11.** B	**12.** C
13. A	**14.** B	**15.** C	**16.** A
17. C	**18.** C	**19.** B	**20.** D

SECTION B

21. (a) maximum turning pt $(-1, 4)$
   minimum turning pt $(1, 0)$

   (b) (i) show $f(1) = 0$

      (ii) $(x - 1)(x - 1)(x + 2)$

   (c)

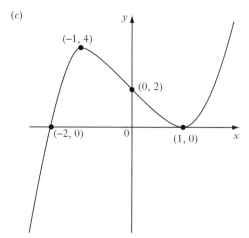

22. (a) $(1, 3)$ and $(3, -3)$

   (b) A $(1, 3)$

23. (a) $h(f(x)) = \log_2(x^2 - x + 10)$
      $h(g(x)) = \log_2(5 - x)$

   (b) $x = 3, -10$

MATHEMATICS HIGHER UNITS 1, 2 AND 3 PAPER 2 2008

1. (a) $m_{BC} = -\dfrac{1}{2}$

   So $m_\perp = 2$
   Midpoint of BC = $(1, -3)$
   so $y + 3 = 2(x - 1)$ leading to
   $y = 2x - 5$

   (b) $y = -3x + 10$

   (c) $(3, 1)$

2. (a) P$(8, 0, 4)$
      Q$(0, 4, 3)$

   (b) $\overrightarrow{PQ} \begin{pmatrix} -8 \\ 4 \\ -1 \end{pmatrix}$ $\overrightarrow{PA} \begin{pmatrix} 0 \\ 0 \\ -4 \end{pmatrix}$

   (c) $83 \cdot 6°$ or $1 \cdot 459$ *radians*

3. (a) (i) $p = \sqrt{7}$

      (ii) $q = -3$

   (b) $\sqrt{7}\cos x - 3\sin x = k \cos x \cos a - k \sin x \sin a$
      so $k \cos a = \sqrt{7}$ *and* $k \sin a = 3$
      $k = 4, a = 0 \cdot 848$
      $4\cos(x + 0 \cdot 848)$

   (c) $-4\sin(x + 0 \cdot 848)$

4. (a) Centre $(-4, -2)$ Radius $\sqrt{58}$

   (b) $d_{centres} = \sqrt{128} \approx 11 \cdot 3$

      sum of radii $= \sqrt{58} + \sqrt{26}$
      $\approx 12 \cdot 7$
      since $12 \cdot 7 > 11 \cdot 3$
      circles touch

   (c) $(3, 1), (-1, 5)$

5. $90°, 199 \cdot 5°, 340 \cdot 5°$

6. (a) ΔOST and ΔRSQ are similar.

   $\therefore \dfrac{QR}{3} = \dfrac{3 - t}{3}$

   and QR $= 6 - 2t$
   (There are other acceptable methods to show that
   QR $= 6 - 2t$)

   (b) Q $= \left(\dfrac{3}{2}, 3\right)$

7. $50\dfrac{2}{3}$

MATHEMATICS HIGHER UNITS 1, 2 AND 3 PAPER 1 (NON-CALCULATOR) 2008 SQP (BASED ON 2004 PAPER)

SECTION A

1. B	**2.** C	**3.** C	**4.** A
5. A	**6.** A	**7.** D	**8.** C
9. C	**10.** A	**11.** A	**12.** D
13. A	**14.** D	**15.** B	**16.** D
17. C	**18.** B	**19.** A	**20.** A

SECTION B

21. (a) maximum at $(-3, 32)$
minimum at $(1, 0)$

(b)

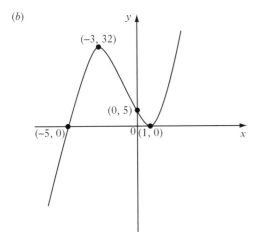

22. $x = 2$

23. $\dfrac{\pi}{6}, \dfrac{\pi}{2}, \dfrac{5\pi}{6}, \dfrac{3\pi}{2}$

24. $-\dfrac{3}{5}$

25. $f(x) = 2x^3 - 6x^2 + 8$

MATHEMATICS HIGHER UNITS 1, 2 AND 3 PAPER 2 2008 SQP (BASED ON 2004 PAPER)

1. $\angle PQR = 72.0°$

2. $b^2 - 4ac = p^2 - 4 \times 2 \times (-3)$
$\qquad\qquad = p^2 + 24$
since p^2 is positive
$b^2 - 4ac \geq 0$ so roots real

3. (a) $x = 2$

(b) $12x - y - 8 = 0$

4. (a) $\sqrt{34} \cos(x - 59)°$

(b) 12.3

5.

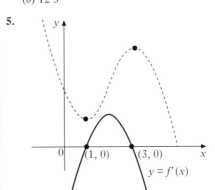

6. (a) A $(6, 1)$

$m_{AP} = 2$ so $m_{PT} = -\dfrac{1}{2}$

$y + 1 = -\dfrac{1}{2}(x - 5)$ so $x + 2y = 3$

(b) $(3 - 2y)^2 + y^2 + 10(3 - 2y) + 2y + 6 = 0$
$5y^2 - 30y + 45 = 0$
$5(y - 3)^2 = 0$.
Repeated roots so line is a tangent.

(c) Q $= (-3, 3)$

PQ $= \sqrt{80}$

7. (a) $A = 2x^2 + 2xh + 4xh = 12$

$V = 2x \cdot x \cdot h$

$= 2x \cdot \dfrac{12 - 2x^2}{6}$

$= 4x - \dfrac{2}{3}x^3 = \dfrac{2}{3}x(6 - x^2)$

(b) $x = \sqrt{2}$

8. (a) 4433

(b) 347 years

9. $\dfrac{2}{3}$ square metres

MATHEMATICS HIGHER
PAPER 1
2009

SECTION A

1. A	2. B	3. D	4. C	5. B
6. A	7. A	8. D	9. A	10. B
11. B	12. C	13. B	14. C	15. A
16. B	17. A	18. D	19. C	20. C

SECTION B

21. (a) P $(-3, 0)$

   (b) $x - 2y + 3 = 0$

   (c) QR. $2x + y - 14 = 0$
      So T $(5, 4)$

22. (a) (i) $\overline{DE} = \begin{pmatrix} -9 \\ 6 \\ 12 \end{pmatrix}$ and $\overline{EF} = \begin{pmatrix} -3 \\ 2 \\ 4 \end{pmatrix}$

   So $\overline{DE} = 3\overline{EF}$

   Since $\overline{DE}$ and $\overline{EF}$ has a common point and a common direction then D, E and F are collinear

   (ii) 3:1

   (b) $\overrightarrow{GE} = \begin{pmatrix} 1-k \\ -3 \\ -3 \end{pmatrix}$ and $\overrightarrow{DE} \cdot \overrightarrow{GE} = 0$

   So $k = 7$.

23. (a)

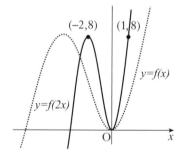

   (b)

24. (a) $\sin\left(\dfrac{7\pi}{12}\right) = \sin\left(\dfrac{\pi}{3} + \dfrac{\pi}{4}\right)$

$= \sin\dfrac{\pi}{3}\ \cos\dfrac{\pi}{4} + \cos\dfrac{\pi}{3}\ \sin\dfrac{\pi}{4}$

$= \dfrac{\sqrt{3}}{2} \times \dfrac{1}{\sqrt{2}} + \dfrac{1}{2} \times \dfrac{1}{\sqrt{2}}$

$= \dfrac{\sqrt{3}+1}{2\sqrt{2}}$

   (b) $\sin(A+B) + \sin(A-B)$

   $= \sin A \cos B + \cos A \sin B + \sin A \cos B - \cos A \sin B$

   $= 2 \sin A \cos B.$

   (c) (i) $\dfrac{\pi}{12} = \dfrac{\pi}{3} - \dfrac{\pi}{4}$

   (ii) $\sin\left(\dfrac{7\pi}{12}\right) + \sin\left(\dfrac{\pi}{12}\right)$

   $= \sin\left(\dfrac{\pi}{3} + \dfrac{\pi}{4}\right) + \sin\left(\dfrac{\pi}{3} - \dfrac{\pi}{4}\right)$

   $= 2 \sin\dfrac{\pi}{3} \cos\dfrac{\pi}{4}$

   $= 2 \times \dfrac{\sqrt{3}}{2} \times \dfrac{1}{\sqrt{2}}$

   $= \dfrac{\sqrt{6}}{2}$

MATHEMATICS HIGHER PAPER 2 2009

1. Maximum turning point at $(-1, 17)$
Minimum turning point at $(3, -15)$

2. (a) (i) $p(x) = 3(x^2 - 2) + 1 = 3x^2 - 5$

(ii) $q(x) = (3x + 1)^2 - 2 = 9x^2 + 6x - 1$

(b) $x = -\dfrac{1}{2}$

3. (a) (i) $f(1) = 1 + 8 + 11 - 20 = 0$ so $x = 1$ is a root

(ii) $(x - 1)(x + 4)(x + 5)$

(b) $\log_2((x + 3)(x^2 + 5x - 4)) = 3$

So $(x + 3)(x^2 + 5x - 4) = 2^3$

$\therefore x^3 + 8x^2 + 11x - 12 = 8$

$\therefore x^3 + 8x^2 + 11x - 20 = 0$

$\therefore (x - 1)(x + 4)(x + 5) = 0$

$x = 1$ or $x - 4$ or $x = -5$

$\therefore x = 1$ only

4. (a) $(5 + 1)^2 + (10 - 2)^2$

$= 6^2 + 8^2$

$= 100 \therefore$ P lies on circle C_1

(b) Q$(-7, -6)$. $M_{RAD} = \dfrac{4}{3}$ so $M_{TANGENT} = -\dfrac{3}{4}$
Eqn of tangent: $3x + 4y + 45 = 0$

(c) Radius of C_2 and C_3 is 20
Centre C_2 (5, 10) so $C_2 : (x - 5)^2 + (y - 10)^2 = 400$
Centre C_3 $(-19, -22)$ so $C_3 : (x + 19)^2 + (y + 22)^2 = 400$.

5. (a) $m = 3, n = 2$

(b) Points of intersection $(0{\cdot}6, 1{\cdot}3)$ and $(2{\cdot}6, 1{\cdot}3)$

(c) $12{\cdot}4$ square units

6. (a) 76 million

(b) $161{\cdot}2$ years

7. (a) $\mathbf{p}\cdot(\mathbf{q} + \mathbf{r}) = 6\sqrt{3}$

$\mathbf{r}\cdot(\mathbf{p} - \mathbf{q}) = \dfrac{9}{4}$

(b) $|\mathbf{q} + \mathbf{r}| = \dfrac{3\sqrt{3}}{2}$

$|\mathbf{p} - \mathbf{q}| = 2{\cdot}05$

MATHEMATICS HIGHER PAPER 1 2010

SECTION A

1. A	2. C	3. D	4. A	5. B
6. D	7. C	8. B	9. C	10. B
11. D	12. A	13. B	14. C	15. C
16. A	17. B	18. B	19. C	20. A

SECTION B

21. (a) $2x + 5y - 72 = 0$

(b) Show that $2 \times 6 + 5 \times 12 - 72 = 0$ so T lies on line BQ.

(c) BT : TQ is 2 : 1

22. (a) $f(x) = (x - 1)(x - 1)(2x + 5)$
or
$f(x) = (x - 1)^2(2x + 5)$

(b) $x = -\dfrac{5}{2}$ **or** $x = 1$

(c) G$(1, -1)$

(d) H$\left(-\dfrac{5}{2}, -8\right)$

23. (a) (i) $m = \dfrac{3}{2}$ and $m = \tan a$ so $\tan a = \dfrac{3}{2}$

(ii) $\sin a = \dfrac{3}{\sqrt{13}}$

(b) $\sin b = \dfrac{3}{5}$ and $\cos b = \dfrac{4}{5}$

(c) (i) $\sin(a - b) = \dfrac{6}{5\sqrt{13}}$

(ii) $\sin(b - a) = -\dfrac{6}{5\sqrt{13}}$

MATHEMATICS HIGHER
PAPER 2
2010

1. (a) M(0, 1, 0) and N(4, 2, 2)

    (b) $\overrightarrow{VM} = \begin{pmatrix} 0 \\ -1 \\ -3 \end{pmatrix}$ and $\overrightarrow{VN} = \begin{pmatrix} 4 \\ 0 \\ -1 \end{pmatrix}$

    (c) $\angle MVN = 76\cdot7°$ **or** $1\cdot339$ radians

2. (a) $k = 13$ and $a = 22\cdot6$ (to 1 d.p.)

    (b) (i) Maximum value 13 and minimum value -13

        (ii) Maximum occurs at $x = 337\cdot4$
              Minimum occurs at $x = 157\cdot4$

3. (a) (i) Substitute expression for y from line into equation of circle
              $$x^2 + (3 - x)^2 + 14x + 4(3 - x) - 19 = 0$$
              leading to $2x^2 + 4x + 2 = 0$ and line being tangent to circle.

        (ii) P(-1, 4)

    (b) $(x - 1)^2 + (y - 6)^2 = 8$

4. $\{2\cdot419, 3\cdot864\}$

5. (a) (i) From T(0, 4), length of PQ is
              $$10 - x^2 - 4 = 6 - x^2$$

        (ii) Area: $2x \times (6 - x^2) = 12x - 2x^3$

    (b) Maxium area $8\sqrt{2}$ ($\approx 11\cdot3$) square units
         (This occurs at $x = \sqrt{2}$ ($\approx 1\cdot4$))

6. (a) From $y = (2x - 9)^{\frac{1}{2}}$ then $m_{\text{tangent}} = \dfrac{dy}{dx} = (2x - 9)^{-\frac{1}{2}}$

         When $x = 9$ then $m_{\text{tangent}} = \dfrac{dy}{dx} = (18 - 9)^{-\frac{1}{2}} = \dfrac{1}{3}$

         and $y = (2x - 9)^{\frac{1}{2}} = (18 - 9)^{\frac{1}{2}} = 3$
         (**NB** Need to use equation of curve to get this value of 3)
         This leads to $y - 3 = \dfrac{1}{3}(x - 9)$ and so $y = \dfrac{1}{3}x$

    (b) $A\left(\dfrac{9}{2}, 0\right)$

    (c) Two main methods:
         Shaded area = area of large triangle $-$ area under curve from $\dfrac{9}{2}$ to 9.
         or
         Shaded area = area of small triangle $+$ area between line and curve from $\dfrac{9}{2}$ to 9.
         This leads to shaded area $\dfrac{9}{2}$ square units.

7. (a) $\log_4 x = P$
         $$x = 4^P$$
         $$\log_{16} x = \log_{16} 4^P$$
         $$= P \log_{16} 4$$
         $$= \dfrac{1}{2}P$$

    (b) $\log_3 x + \log_9 x = 12$
         $$\log_3 x + \dfrac{1}{2}\log_3 x = 12$$
         $$\dfrac{3}{2}\log_3 x = 12$$
         $$\log_3 x = 8$$
         $$x = 3^8 \quad (6561)$$

MATHEMATICS HIGHER
PAPER 1
2011

SECTION A

1. C	2. B	3. D	4. D	5. A
6. C	7. D	8. A	9. B	10. D
11. D	12. C	13. C	14. B	15. B
16. A	17. A	18. C	19. C	20. D

SECTION B

21. (a) $3x - y - 9 = 0$

    (b) E(5, 6)

    (c) (i) $2x + y - 16 = 0$

        (ii) e.g. Substitute E(5, 6) into $2x + y - 16$ and show the result is 0

22. (a) (i) (2, 0)

        (ii) (0, -2)

    (b) Maximum turning point at $\left(\dfrac{1}{3}, -\dfrac{50}{27}\right)$

         Minimum turning point at (1, -2)

    (c) (i)

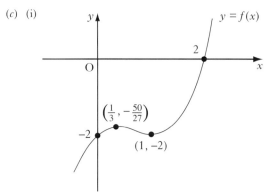

        (ii)

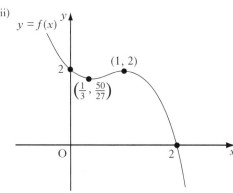

23. (a) $\{0, 60, 300\}$

    (b) Using the fact $\cos 4x = \cos(2 \times 2x)$
         leading to $\{0, 30, 150, 180, 210, 330\}$

MATHEMATICS HIGHER
PAPER 2
2011

1. (a) B(4, 4, 0)

    (b) $\overrightarrow{DB} = \begin{pmatrix} 2 \\ 2 \\ -6 \end{pmatrix}$ and $\overrightarrow{DM} = \begin{pmatrix} 0 \\ -2 \\ -6 \end{pmatrix}$

    (c) $40.3°$ or 0.703 rads

2. (a) $g(f(x)) = g(x^3 - 1)$
                  $= 3x^3 - 2$

    (b) $g(f(x)) + xh(x) = 3x^3 - 2 + 4x^2 - 5x$
                             $= 3x^3 + 4x^2 - 5x - 2$

    (c) $(x - 1)(3x + 1)(x + 2)$

    (d) $\left\{ -2, -\dfrac{1}{3}, 1 \right\}$

3. (a) $u_1 = 8$ and $u_2 = -4$

    (b) $p = 2$ and $q = -3$

    (c) (i) Limit is 0.

         (ii) 2 lies outside the interval $-1 < a < 1$, where $a = 2$

4. Shaded area: $\displaystyle\int_{-2}^{0} (x^3 - x^2 - 4x + 4) - (2x + 4)\, dx +$

                       $\displaystyle\int_{0}^{3} (2x + 4) - (x^3 - x^2 - 4x + 4)\, dx$

                       $= \dfrac{253}{12}$

5. $k = 32$ and $n = \dfrac{1}{2}$

6. (a) $R = \sqrt{34}$ and $a = 5.253$

    (b) $t = 0.6$

7. $-23 < p < 13$

Hey! I've done it

© 2011 SQA/Bright Red Publishing Limited, All Rights Reserved
Published by Bright Red Publishing Ltd, 6 Stafford Street, Edinburgh, EH3 7AU
Tel: 0131 220 5804, Fax: 0131 220 6710, enquiries: sales@brightredpublishing.co.uk,
www.brightredpublishing.co.uk

Official SQA answers to 978-1-84948-221-9
2007-2011